ↄ

Reemerging Russia
Search for Identity

**A Humanities Program on the History,
Culture and Current Dilemmas
of the Russian People**

OASIS

Edited by

**Max J. Okenfuss
Cheryl D. Roberts**

Simon & Schuster
Custom Publishing

Reemerging Russia: Search for Identity is an original publication.

Major funding support provided by The National Endowment for the Humanities, Public Humanities Projects, Washington, D.C.

To receive additional information on The OASIS Institute programs, write 7710 Carondelet Avenue, Suite 125, St. Louis, Missouri 63105, or call 314–862–2933.

Cover design by The Falk Design Group, St. Louis, Missouri
Illustration by Jonathan Evans, St. Louis, Missouri

Printed in the United States of America

10 9 8 7 6 5 4 3 2 1

ISBN 0–536–58740-X
BA 5572

 SIMON & SCHUSTER CUSTOM PUBLISHING
160 Gould Street/Needham Heights, MA 02194
Simon & Schuster Higher Education Publishing Group

COPYRIGHT ACKNOWLEDGMENTS

Table of Contents

Foreword

In 1993, Russia was identified by OASIS members participating in focus groups as their first choice of topics for new programs. As with many ideas, the metamorphosis from concept to finished product has been enlightening and enriching. Thanks to the involvement of many talented and committed people, the OASIS Institute is pleased to provide this anthology of original essays as part of the *Reemerging Russia: Search for Identity* program.

Reemerging Russia: Search for Identity brings together humanities scholars and older Americans nationwide in a series of ten forums to explore this timely topic. The project's director, historian Max Okenfuss of Washington University in St. Louis, and Cheryl Roberts, the project coordinator, have worked closely with the scholars to produce the anthology and video materials for the ten-session program. In some of the OASIS cities, these forums will be enriched by additional film and book discussion series and an intergenerational program involving high school students and older adults. Everyone who participates in the program brings a distinctive perspective shaped by history, the media, and their personal experiences, thus dynamically reshaping it each time it is offered throughout the country.

While the lives of most Americans have been touched by events in the Soviet Union, each of us remembers different things. Some may remember the controversy over diplomatic recognition of the USSR in the 1920s, or the dreams of a rational society at the time of the first Five-Year-Plans in the 1920s. Most will remember the uneasy alliance between the Soviet Union and the United

States during World War II, and the even more precarious stance during the Cold War. Others may recall the revelations about Stalinism, the image of Khrushchev banging his shoe in the United Nations, or the Cuban missile crisis. Many will remember President Nixon's first visit to Moscow, the scandal over Pasternak's Nobel Prize, or the defections of Solzhenitsyn and Nureyev. Indeed, the political history of the USSR and its relations with the United States have had an impact on everyone.

Now all of that has changed. In the past few years, Communism has been rejected as the national ideology across Eurasia, the Soviet military and economic systems in Eastern Europe have disintegrated, and the Soviet Union has been dismembered. The "curtain" is down. We now have an unprecedented opportunity to put aside the political concerns of the Cold War and ask questions about the lives and aspirations of the Russian people.

Reemerging Russia provides a unique opportunity for public audiences to examine Russia's history, literature, art, cinema, and social issues in order to develop a clearer understanding of the ethnicity, religious values, social ideals, and current dilemmas of the Russian people.

Russians today are questioning their old identities. They are asking questions about the role of their former tsars, about traditional Russian peasant values, and about the constitutional institutions that governed their national life. Many Russians are challenging the roles assigned to women and the family in socialist society. At every level they are now asking who they are, what their nation should become, and what their role in the world ought to be. This search for identity is the focus of *Reemerging Russia*.

For over a decade, OASIS has brought the humanities to the public. Our mission is to enrich the cultural, social, and physical quality of life for older adults. Offering challenging programs in the humanities, the arts, volunteer service, and health maintenance, OASIS creates opportunities for individuals over fifty-five to continue their intellectual and personal growth, as well as their involvement in the community.

Our purpose is to make innovative programs, such as *Reemerging Russia*, available to a broad audience. OASIS was initially funded by a grant from the Department of Health and Human Services, Administration on Aging, to demonstrate the feasibility of a public/private partnership. Our major national sponsor is The May Department Stores Company. May Company support is augmented in each OASIS city by other national corporations and local sponsors, generally including a local nonprofit organization, such as the Area Agency on Aging or Department of Aging, and a hospital or other health care provider.

With dedicated educational centers in twenty-five cities across the nation, and serving an expanding membership of over 200,000 adults, OASIS is a national organization with resources uniquely suited to offer this program. We look forward to the interaction and discussion between humanities scholars and audiences. It is this dialogue that will truly enrich the program, taking it beyond the limited bounds of any text or video, to enhance the participants' awareness of this always changing and challenging world.

Marylen Mann
Executive Director
The OASIS Institute

Acknowledgments

This anthology was produced by The OASIS Institute of St. Louis as part of the *Reemerging Russia: Search for Identity* program. We wish to thank and acknowledge the following for their role in making this program possible:

Special thanks to the National Endowment for the Humanities, Public Humanities Projects for their major funding support and commitment to this program.

Additional thanks go to our co-sponsors: BJC Health System, Higher Education Center of St. Louis, International Education Consortium, The May Department Stores Company, Missouri Humanities Council, The Jewish Hospital of St. Louis, The Saint Louis Art Museum, The Saint Louis Public Library, and Washington University in St. Louis.

The transformation from idea to reality happens when committed individuals work together to do whatever it takes to get the job done. The following individuals did just that. Sincere appreciation goes to Max Okenfuss, director of the Reemerging Russia project, and Cheryl Roberts, project coordinator, for their time, expertise and creativity; Marylen Mann, Executive Director of The OASIS Institute, for her vision and enthusiastic dedication; Janice Branham, OASIS Director of Communications and Finance, for her critical role in planning and development; the authors of these original essays, not just for their writing, but for all their contributions to the program; Glen Holt, Judy Simms and Diane Freiermuth for the book discussion series at the Central Library; Dan Reich for the film series at the Art Museum; Sam Wood and Nancy Munshaw, Higher Education Center, for video production; Louise Losos for adding *Reemerging Russia* (and older adults) to her sophomore history class at Ladue Horton Watkins High School; The Falk Design Group, particularly Ken Keuhnel for his patience and creativity; artist Jonathan Evans for his expressive illustration; the Advisory Committee: Gladys Barker, Fanny Bryan, Carol Cradock, Lorraine Glazar, Karen Kessler, Thea Neal, Roger Ray, Christine Reilly, Renata Rotkowicz, Daniel Schlafly, Daniel Shilling, Terry Williams, and Shirley Wink; Marsha Clark and Brian Stephenson, St. Louis OASIS Center; the OASIS staff and volunteers, particularly Jo Baker, Betty Hayes, Mary Jo Rehg, Karen Safe, Deneen Sneed, Verna Smith, and Beverly Zimmerman; and all those who participated in transforming this timely idea into an insightful program.

ఇర

The Humanist Vision of Russia

Richard Stites

Georgetown University, Washington, D.C.

New Ways of Looking at Russia

The humanities scholars who contributed to this volume are concerned with the ideas and realities of ordinary people, especially the Russian people and some of their neighbors. These scholars represent a growing alliance between cultural and social history that aspires to make Russian studies accessible to large numbers of interested persons of every age.

This program offers an examination of Russia that is more than a dull parade of leaders and their politics. It goes beyond the ferocious struggles that have engaged them in war, peace, and revolution. Its objective is to broaden and humanize history by dealing with real people—their emotions and dreams. *Reemerging Russia* introduces Americans to the life of ordinary Russian people by looking at family and work values, religious beliefs, and cultural tastes. By joining the study of politics with the study of *high culture*—fine art, classical music, legitimate theater, ballet, opera and classical studies—and *popular culture*—urban culture produced for a mass audience—we hope to illuminate the inner lives of the dwellers of that immense country.

Are Russians human? This may seem like an absurd question. It is not meant to suggest that Americans ever held Russians to be inhuman, though some of our propaganda and popular culture did convey such images in the worst times of the Cold War. It does suggest, however, that for a long time, most of us simply ignored the human character of the Russian people. Many Americans will confess, some regretfully, to having very little understanding of Soviet society and its essential humanity. The main reason for this was the long-time masking of real life in that part of the world. This was partially the work of suspicious Soviet officials who hid much of the reality behind official walls—a tradition that goes back to old tsarist practices of covering poverty and ugliness with a glossy front. This practice, not unique to Russia, arose out of national pride and out of a belief that most foreigners, if allowed to gaze on the Russian way of life, would only scorn it. The fear was justified. In the 1830s, a German innkeeper uttered these words about Russian travelers.

> When they come through here on their way to Europe they have a gay, free, happy air. . . . The same people, on their return, have long gloomy, tormented faces; they have a worried look. Their conversation is brief and their speech abrupt. I have concluded from this difference that a country which one leaves with so much joy and returns to with so much regret is a bad country.

In manipulating the reality available to foreigners, Russian and Soviet officials often succeeded in hiding both the attractive and the negative sides of their world. American scholars and commentators were guilty of the same thing. The wide and careless use of terms like "totalitarianism" or "evil empire" led most Americans not only to ignore values and customs of Russian and Soviet peoples, but to fear them. Of course, under Stalin, the leaders really did hope to control life, enforce conformity, and remake Soviet humanity. They never succeeded in this, despite propaganda, brutal police forces, and slave labor camps.

In the West, totalitarian theorists sometimes exaggerated the state's power to produce complete obedience. They seemed to suggest that Soviet leaders were capable of achieving total uniformity of thought and behavior among millions of people.

American's educated opinion of the Soviet Union was also shaped by journalists and "Kremlinologists" who often described the Soviet Union as some kind of machine ruling over millions of robotic slaves permanently locked in fear. For ordinary Americans, the picture was further distorted in novels like George Orwell's *1984* and by Cold-War anti-communist films. In these films, "Russians" were portrayed as unsmiling communists—either actively cruel or helplessly passive. The resulting attitude was: Why study Soviet society when it is merely an extension of the state? Why study its culture when it is merely propaganda? Why study its values when none exist outside the official communist ideology of the state?

The true picture of the Russian people was in the past and is today far more complex and interesting. No one can deny the horrors and suffering heaped upon millions by the state under Stalin, nor the Party's attempt to reshape personalities and institutions. The population of the USSR endured an almost unprecedented battering in the midst of the great wars, revolutions, collectivization, and purges of the twentieth century, as discussed in Professor Okenfuss' essay.

Through all these challenges, however, most people tried to live normal lives. They worked, studied, flirted, courted, married, and raised families. Patriots loved and served and died for their country. Ambitious individuals tried to move upward on the economic ladder and to provide for their loved ones. After the death of Stalin, a great deal of fear disappeared. His successors Khrushchev, Brezhnev, and the others in political power, for all of their faults and errors, made everyday life much easier for the Soviet people. Life was full of drama and melodrama, failure and achievements, betrayal and heroism, nastiness and exalted pleasure, laughter and tears. All of this was reflected, however dimly, in the songs, movies, novels, radio shows, and television programs that Soviets have always avidly enjoyed. However much they welcomed the new cultural freedoms, when the communist system collapsed, millions of Russians looked back on "the good old days" of Soviet power as a time when their lives had been stable, orderly, and predictable.

The reform of a reemerging Russia will be shaped by its people. The current dilemmas will be resolved in ways that no one can foresee. Now it is important to ask *first what* is and then define *what may* be. To understand the Russia of today, we must learn what things are really like, what people feel and think about issues, what historical background forged their reactions to the present moment. What are the deep values, customs, and beliefs of the Russian people that may foster or impede the flowering of democracy, a free market, and normal relations with each other and their neighbors? What would drive them to allow a return to authoritarian rule or nationalism?

Search for Identity

The people of Moscow, Vladivostok, and a thousand other towns, villages and farm settlements in the vast Russian Federation are undergoing a profound crisis of identity. They are genuinely puzzled about where they came from, who they are, and how they can live together in a dizzying new order. A nation's history is part of its bloodstream. We Americans are constantly reinventing ourselves and reshaping the notion of what an "American" is. Still we have a strong sense of where we came from and, in spite of great injustices that have scarred our past, a sense of pride. In recent years Russians have heard the shattering news that their recent past has been a barbaric myth. Not only from foreign informants, but their own intellectual leaders have told them that they have been lied to. They have read it in newspapers and novels, watched it on television and in films. The message beneath it all is that Russians have no twentieth century history to be proud of—that the revolution, socialism, Lenin, and the Soviet system were all part of a big mistake, a colossal tragedy. Older men and women who worked to build their country's industries in the 1930s, who fought against Nazi Germany in the 1940s, who lived, loved and labored through the decades, are now expected to look back on their whole lives as pieces of the *great lie* and the *great crime* of Soviet history. Younger people are ashamed of their parents' lives. They have no foundation on which to build, no sense that their dreams can change their reality. So they abandon dreams, as Professor Vishevsky elaborates in his essay.

Some of this historical nay-saying has been grossly exaggerated, denying any real Soviet achievements and glorifying all of tsarist history—the era that preceded the Russian Revolution of 1917. Russian critics and scholars have done an intellectual somersault. Those recently paid and forced by the State to glorify everything Soviet and curse everything Western are now doing the opposite. Ordinary Russians are split on this matter. Some angrily deny the "new history," others endorse it, still others feel puzzled by it. One of the great tasks in rebuilding national identity is the sober reassessment of history through the lens of common sense, perspective, and factual honesty.

The sense of "national character" has been weakened also by the breakup of the empire and by the bitter realities of cultural diversity outlined in Professor Batalden's essay. The Union of Soviet Socialist Republics, composed of 15 different national republics, was a multinational state, or empire, as some have called it. In the USSR, as in the pre-revolutionary Russian empire, the Russians always saw themselves as the dominant nationality, the leading cultural force of that great patchwork of peoples. Russian leaders often abused their powers over the non-Russian, Central Asian Muslims, the peoples of the Caucasus, non-Russian Slavs, Jews, and many others. Yet many Russians were surprised and upset when these people, having fallen away from Moscow after the collapse of the USSR in 1991, turned the ugly face of resentment toward them. Russians thought they had sacrificed and toiled to educate and help modernize these peoples. The dismay of the Russians has been worsened by two very real and potentially inflammatory problems: Russians in the outlying republics—the *near abroad*—and non-Russians in the heartland. The first case is well-known: millions of ethnic Russians, Ukrainians and Belorussians still live in non-Russian republics where they are sometimes treated as second-class citizens. In the lesser known case, thousands of refugees from war-torn corners of the old USSR have come to Moscow and other cities to seek survival and shelter. In doing so, they compete for scarce jobs, housing, and resources. Russians are not above racially motivated resentments similar to those of Germans toward foreign guest workers or of white U.S. auto workers in Detroit fifty years ago toward

Blacks. Since some newcomers are shady dealers at best or out-right gangsters at worst, the resentment turns to fear and rage. In times of economic stress, the appearance of successful Georgian, Armenian, or Jewish businessmen under the new capitalism complicates already uneasy feelings of who will be who in the new Russia. Some of this ethnic tension is inevitable in a transforming society, but this abstract sociological fact does not provide much balm for injured national self-esteem and wounded feelings.

Another new stress-line in the emerging society is the changing status of women. As Professor Clements' essay illustrates, this subject is filled with conflicts of myth and reality. The Russian Revolution introduced many novel and progressive benefits to women in the Soviet Union. After the initial flush of liberationist laws and slogans, a less traditional but still patriarchal gender-system took root—a blend of old-fashioned customs and state-sponsored role assignments. Women had to work, to bear and raise children, do most of the housework, accept the husband as master, and be satisfied with second class jobs. The prevailing sexual culture and appalling medical practices brought much abuse of women. The enormous loss of male lives in World War II left many women without husbands and led many others to accept marriage on unfavorable terms. Thus, the censure of the regime and its neglect of domestic amenities added up to a mammoth burden on the average woman.

Russia is in the midst of startling changes in gender roles. The surprising electoral showing of a women's party in a 1993 parliamentary vote hints at the change. Political activity of women is, of course, no guarantee that deeper social transformations will occur. Russian feminists organized themselves and fought for the vote back in the years of the last tsar (1905–1917) but without major social change for the masses of women. In the Soviet period, women had no independent political organizations. Women's consciousness now seems much more powerful than in earlier times. It is operating in a context of other freedoms, reforms, and immense upheavals. In a country where the unthinkable is now thinkable (if not always doable), the notion of a dynamic women's movement with political weight and social

Future feminist? Traditional Soviet society and culture rewarded women who excelled in sports and the arts. How much will the unleashing of Russian popular taste influence the old nurturing of high culture?

(Independent Newspaper from Russia, Inc.)

consequences is becoming widely accepted. The new feminists have plugged into the worldwide feminist movement. Russian women leaders have a very broad and realistic view of how to get things done and how much can be done. Their voices—short of a right-wing backlash—will not be silenced as they have been in the past.

Demands for a greater role for women in the workplace, in politics, and in the family have their own special fallout. Men in Russia, like those elsewhere in the world, feel disoriented and threatened or resentful. The "gender menace" is like the "ethnic menace." It changes the rules, shifts roles, and dissolves old identities and certainties. Because of this, many Russian women— perhaps even most—are also suspicious of the feminist wave, fearing the loss of their familiar codes of femininity. Since Gorbachev's introduction of *glasnost´* or openness, shocking public displays of sexuality have raised anxiety about the future of the family and of conventional morality.

Aggravating the decay of the economy, the loss of empire, and the frightening crime rate, are the mental and emotional apprehensions of the Russian people, apprehensions that come from a feeling of loss—a loss of status, of identity, and of a world in which, even with all its injustices and deprivations, people had learned to live.

The Influence of Religion

Religion is not only a system of faith and an organized church. It is also a collection of rituals and shared values that can help define the devotional and spiritual lives of a people. It is a central feature of "culture" in the broad meaning of the word and has played a boundless role in the history of the Russian people, particularly the rural masses. But beginning in the 18th century, many among the upper classes fell away from their Orthodox faith and embraced a more secular view of the world. Almost all of the radicals and revolutionary socialists were atheists, as were the Marxist Bolsheviks or Communists who came to power in 1917. As discussed in Dr. Garrard's essay, the Bolsheviks actively struggled against religion, sometimes ferociously, killing priests, smashing icons, and destroying ancient churches. Although there were times when they were more moderate, they were always constant in terms of not allowing religion to be part of any educational experience—formal or otherwise.

Russians are now positioned at various places on a complex continuum. On one end of the continuum are those who are rebuilding the church and trying to spread its values. On the other end are those who proclaim a secular world based on science and reason. In between these two groups are many who ambivalently share or disbelieve both of these positions and who are struggling to understand how their feelings and beliefs fit into the emerging identity.

Society Through the Creative Eye

Let us turn to "culture" in the more conventional sense—the human experience and imagination crystallized in works of art and artifact. The essays by Professors Weil, Vishevsky, Carlson, and Youngblood clarify the impressive roles played by literature, art, and cinema in Russian life, past and present. But art is both created and consumed. For example, both the writer and popular taste are equally important as barometers of national mood. In these essays, my colleagues hope to provoke questioning, doubts, and disagreements among our readers and listeners by dwelling both on high culture and the tastes of ordinary people. This approach should reveal the complexity of the real world.

Why study popular culture? High culture and the classics address the eternal truths, the deepest values, and the big questions. But people also operate on the basis of "superficial" values and the ephemeral trends of the time. These are reflected in the popular culture which rarely concerns itself with the great enigmas of human experience. The study of popular culture, like any other intellectual enterprise, can descend into a hobby such as beer-can collecting. But light can emanate from below as well as from above. Patterns of popular taste reflect, among other things, attitudes about the city, the state, the nation, the family, money, foreigners, minorities, the arts, and the "system." The consumption of culture is part of a people's biography. Popular culture, i.e. the types of movies people prefer to see for entertainment, can be a means of bonding for most people in a way that high culture cannot.

Popular culture usually means culture produced for a mass audience—rock concerts, movies, dining out, and other forms of entertainment. It is not only contemporary but very often temporary. It is therefore distinct from the fine arts, theatre, ballet, opera and classical studies of high culture. It is also different from folk culture which is produced in the countryside by peasants. In Russia, as elsewhere, there has been an exchange among these levels of culture, fueled largely by increased literacy, urbanization and technology during the last century.

In the Russian empire, the rise of popular culture was driven by social and economic transformations at the turn of the century: the introduction of a mass press; the importation of photographic, cinematic, and phonographic techniques; the arrival of European and American entertainment (music hall, revue, cabaret, ragtime, tango, the motion picture); the spread of restaurants and cafés. Education and literacy brought about a general shift in reading and entertainment habits of the lower and lower-middle classes of the towns. In the last decades of the Old Regime, popular culture was reflected in songs, sheet music, stage shows, pulp and boulevard fiction, and movies. The most popular single genre of mass entertainment was the movie melodrama. Although many educated people criticized popular entertainment on the grounds of good taste and decency, neither they nor the tsarist censorship did much to curb it.

All this changed in the Soviet period. After a few years of confusion and absence of a coherent policy, the regime nationalized practically the entire popular entertainment industry: movie studios, the stage, circus, the press, and public performance. Then government control diminished during the New Economic Policy (NEP) of the 1920s. The partial resurgence of "vulgar" commercial entertainment revealed that the urban masses, when given a

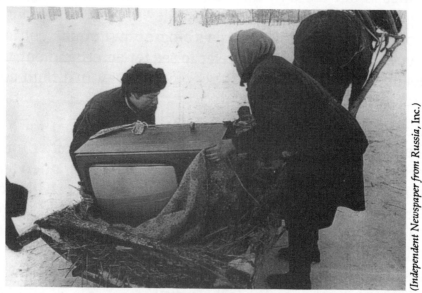

(Independent Newspaper from Russia, Inc.)

Old and new: a Russian collective-farm family unloads their new purchase.

choice, preferred it over the revolutionary heroics of Bolshevik artists. In cinema, for example, as noted in Professor Youngblood's essay, they preferred comedy, adventure, intrigue, and crime stories with clear plots, strong characters, and plenty of action. These "escapist" movies were preferred over the high-culture spectacles of great film-makers like Eisenstein.

In the 1930s a Stalinist system of "mass" culture based on socialist realism was established. This lasted in a rigid form (except for the wartime period) until Stalin's death in 1953, and in many of its essential forms until the advent of *glasnost'* (openness) and *perestroika* (restructuring) around 1985-86. Stalinist mass culture—rooted in the values of the political elite, but expanded by a need to reach the masses—excluded sexual and mystical-religious themes. It also discouraged experimental or avant-garde forms. Instead it offered realistic representation, the worship of state leaders, and the values of socialist construction, revolutionary adventure, and optimism. From this came hundreds of songs for youth, workers, and soldiers; an elaborate system of folk ensembles; a politically correct comedy stage and circus arena; tales of aviation, exploration, public-works construction, and defense; and musical comedy films which combined entertainment, lavish production, and heavy-handed social messages. Lyubov Orlova, the film star, became one of the cultural icons of the age remembered by millions down to the present, though she was virtually unknown outside the USSR.

Soviet popular culture reached a level of maturity and accommodation in the Khrushchev and Brezhnev decades. A continued prohibition of the forbidden themes was combined with a loosening up on Western cultural imports. In this era, the great stars of mass Soviet culture emerged: Alla Pugacheva, the queen of popular song; Arkadii Raikin, the king of stage satire; Oleg Popov, the circus clown; Eldar Ryazanov, the film comedy director; and Iulian Semenov, the master of the spy thriller. These artists enjoyed immense popularity not only in live performance and in print, but also on television. Their works were consumed on a mass scale and they themselves became national celebrities and household words. The great art produced in the concert halls, the

(Independent Newspaper from Russia, Inc.)

Erotica in Russia. Without traditional censorship, people are faced with making their own judgments and rules. A recent survey of Russian residents revealed that 34% believe distributors of erotic films and literature should not be punished, 13% say they should be fined, 10% believe they should be imprisoned, 27% weren't sure, and 16% confessed they did not know the meaning of words like "erotica" or "pornography."

ballet, opera, dramatic theaters, and the great literary magazines could not compete with the popular arts in terms of mass appeal. Elitist bias, cultural diplomacy, and ignorance of people's tastes and preferences led Western observers to ignore the vast realm of popular culture. Outsiders were led to believe that the artists, musicians, and writers known to the outside world were automatically the favorites of Soviet citizens, as well. Thus American observers, who were taught to identify Russian tastes with the Bolshoi Ballet, were astonished to discover that millions of viewers—when given the choice—infinitely preferred to watch "ten handkerchief" soap operas and adventure movies.

Since 1985, the old structures of state-sponsored culture have all but collapsed and new organisms are feeding the tastes of the younger generation. Rock music, films of sex and violence, cheap foreign imports, and music video are on the cutting edge of popular culture. The censorship, firmly in place for more than fifty years, is virtually gone. Old-style big bands and crooners, folk groups, political or ideological films, and cause-promoting plays are being nudged off stage and screen—movies, television and videos—in favor of entertainment that contains the novelty and shock effect that the younger generation of Soviet citizens crave. Since older persons continue to cherish the cultural forms of their youth (war songs and movies for example), the generational tension that has always existed has taken on sharp forms, sometimes expressed in ideological and political language. Conservative nationalist Russians or Russophiles have taken particular offense at the provocative gestures, clothing, music, and lyrics of certain rock singers and bands. Thus popular culture, virtually ignored in Soviet scholarship of the past, has now surfaced as a visible social and political phenomenon. It is a barometer, however mercurial, of Russian moods and desires.

A New Vision: Future, Past, Present

Let me conclude with a few words about the future and how best to look at it. I began by saying that grappling with the reality of a people is not fostered by looking only at their politics or economic system. I hope these essays demonstrate, as they have forcefully tried to do, how

Some have suggested that the government's inability to control the influx of Western pop and rock music did as much to destroy the Soviet Union as the arms race. At a recent rock concert, young people displayed their enthusiasm for the end of censorship.

(Independent Newspaper from Russia, Inc.)

utterly important it is for both individuals and nations to reach out across the multiple chasms that separate them in a search for genuine understanding and empathy. To do this, everyone one must look carefully at the past and the present. This does not mean we have to agree with the other or even like what they do. It does mean trying to empathize with some of their dilemmas and choices, agonies and hopes. To see the other not as a faceless mass of either enemies or pitiable victims, but complex human beings like us, but who are coming out of a historical and cultural experience which has been both glorious and tragic in its special, historically conditioned way. It is no longer possible to look at Russians as the people behind the daily headlines, but rather as part of our world. Let us hope that they are now learning to look at us in new ways as well.

Suggested Readings

Billington, James. *The Icon and the Axe*. New York: Knopf, 1966.

Buckley, Mary. *Perestroika and Soviet Women*. Cambridge: Cambridge University Press, 1992.

Hosking, Geoffrey. *The Awakening of Russia*. Cambridge, MA: Harvard University Press, 1990.

Kenez, Peter. *Cinema in Soviet Society 1917–1953*. Cambridge: Cambridge University Press, 1992.

Lawton, Anna. *Kinoglasnost: Soviet Cinema in Our Time*. Cambridge: Cambridge University Press, 1992.

Remnick, David. *Lenin's Tomb*. New York: Random House, 1993.

Riordan, James. *Soviet Youth Culture*. Bloomington: Indiana University Press, 1989.

Stites, Richard. *Revolutionary Dreams*. Oxford: Oxford University Press, 1989.

Stites, Richard. *Russian Popular Culture*. Cambridge: Cambridge University Press, 1992.

Youngblood, Denise. *Movies for the Masses*. Cambridge: Cambridge University Press, 1992.

இ

Russia's Twentieth-Century Revolutions

Max J. Okenfuss

Washington University, St. Louis, Missouri

Russia Enters the Twentieth Century

Twentieth-century Russia was born of many revolutions. Most of us think only of the Bolshevik Revolution of 1917, but Russia's revolutions were far more numerous and complex than Lenin's seizure of power. They spanned the whole fabric of Russian life.

The Social Revolution

Until 1861, Russian intellectuals viewed the Russian peasants' religious faith, communal decision-making, and hardy self-reliance as the essence of Russianness. Then a massive social revolution began with the liberation of the Russian serfs. Millions of Russian peasants, who had previously belonged to individual nobles or to the state, obtained their personal freedom and acquired civil rights. Unlike the American slaves who were freed without land, Russian peasants who had farmed the land were guaranteed permanent access to it. Indeed the peasants remained bound to their villages, as authorities tried to minimize exodus to the cities. They wanted the majority of Russian peasants to remain on their customary lands, and to minimize any disturbance to traditional village life and leadership.

The end of serfdom meant the end of a justice system controlled by the Russian nobility. Consequently, land reform was, of necessity, followed by judicial reform. Trial by jury, a legal profession, and legal protection were all introduced. Suddenly the noble's control over the countryside was gone, and a transformation of local government was required. In theory, Russia's peasants could now participate with nobles in electing their local government. These new rural administrations, and their parallel institutions in the cities of Russia, proved willing and able to govern themselves. They were also willing to tax themselves. They invested in roads and bridges, in public health, and especially in education. The basis for a modern social revolution had been created by emancipation in 1861. With that revolution, popular culture arose, taking its place alongside the peasant culture and the high culture of Russia's elite, the world of Tolstoy and Dostoyevsky, and of the famous composers.

The Economic Revolution

The next revolution was an economic one. It began a generation later with rapid government-sponsored industrialization, especially in coal, iron, steel, and railway transportation. In the 1890's, under the leadership of Sergei Witte, the Minister of Finance and former railroad entrepreneur, the Russian government committed itself to the kind of industrial growth pioneered in Western Europe a century earlier. Governmental initiatives raised taxes in order to cut back consumption, and invested the revenue in industry. Foreign investment was encouraged, and the government channeled resources into heavy industry and railroad construction. A new working class was created. Small by European standards, it was concentrated in a few industrialized regions. Because wages were often low and working conditions poor, socialists easily indoctrinated the new working class. Consequently, the increase in national industrial output was accompanied by increased social tensions.

In the end, these reforms brought Russia economically into the modern world. Everywhere the guiding force was the government. So intense was its involvement and so extensive its ownership of new enterprises that some commentators referred to a nationalized or "socialist" economy long before the Bolsheviks seized power. Ultimately, the result of modernization was the creation of more diversity among the Russian population, and a crisis of identity for many.

The Russia that absorbed these modern social and economic revolutions was already a vast, multi-ethnic, multi-cultural, multi-religious empire. By the time the European imperialist powers began their rapid empire-building in tropical and sub-tropical parts of the globe, the Russians had already established and extended their control over large segments of eastern Europe and central Asia. By 1870, the Russians controlled the Finns, Belorussians, Lithuanians, and Poles in the northwest and west, the Romanians and Ukrainians in the southwest, and the Georgians, Armenians, and the myriad of peoples of the Caucasus and Caspian lands to the south. They dominated the vast expanses and peoples of Islamic central Asia and pagan Siberia. Only in America did Russia retreat from this centuries' old pattern of expansion, withdrawing from Alaska and the Pacific northwest.

On paper this vast nation was officially a Russian-speaking, Orthodox Christian population that had been ruled autocratically since 1613 by a Christian emperor of the House of Romanov. In reality, it was a diverse realm of many peoples, religions, and languages. Russia was loosely administered by a patchwork of governors, regional nobilities, and semi-independent local officials. As social and economic change swept the empire at the beginning of the twentieth century, many Russians responded with the politics of reaction and conservatism, seeking to preserve the old ways. The conservatives rejected needless innovations from the West, and blamed Russia's agonies on a variety of scapegoats. The infamous massacres and Russian anti-semitic pogroms of the early twentieth century were part of this religious redefinition of an increasingly complex Russian reality.

The Political Revolution

In 1905 this enormous structure nearly collapsed as a political revolution shook the nation and the regime to their foundations. There were urban food riots everywhere. The population had doubled in the preceding half-century, and over-taxed, sullen peasants were struggling to support two families on land that had previously supported only one. The peasants rebelled, and the government was forced to reduce their taxes and other financial obligations. The army and navy—now largely comprised of peasants forced into service—engaged in an unpopular war with Japan. This resulted in mutinies. The new urban industrial working class, often comprised of single males who were isolated from their families and villages, went on strike. University professors and students protested. A developing middle-class, newly organized into all-Russian associations of lawyers, engineers, doctors, teachers and other professionals, wrote petitions denouncing the government. Perhaps most ominously, in an age of European nation-building, the scores of national minorities began to talk of secession and independence. One by one they began to rediscover and resurrect native languages and cultures which were distinct from those of their Russian masters.

These revolutions forced the tsarist government to issue a constitution. It promised an elective legislature or Duma, and limited the powers of the emperor. This promise of a constitutional monarchy gained a respite for the Romanovs. Indeed, things quieted down so quickly that the last tsar, Nicholas II, soon felt that he had conceded too much.

The new constitution did not completely alter the face of the Russian empire, nor did it satisfy the regime's many opponents. So many groups and voices had been arrayed against the tsar that no single program or party would satisfy all. The result of these divisions was the appearance of a host of political parties that vied for representation in the new national legislature, the Duma. Their bickering, and Nicholas' unwillingness to share power with the Duma, did not bode well for democracy in Russia.

Russia's Cultural Revolution

Beyond the social, economic and political revolutions, there was another which is often forgotten and unappreciated. Like Europe, Russia before the First World War also experienced a cultural revolution, a sudden explosion in the humanities and arts. The political revolutions of 1905 aided this cultural revolution by ending the censorship that had controlled the printing press in the nineteenth century.

In literature, this was Russia's Silver Age. The Golden Age had produced great novelists of realism: the mid-nineteenth-century world of Turgenev, Dostoevsky, Tolstoy, and Goncharov. Now Russian presses produced the works of poets, symbolists, and futurists. They were unconventional, rebellious in form, and escapist in sentiment. Contemptuous of elite and middle-class values, some abolished rhyme, meter, and even punctuation. Some praised disorder and held the past in contempt. These new authors mocked religion and the past giants of Russian literature. They demanded the right to use words anyway they chose. The poet Mayakovsky began a poem with the words: *I like watching children die.*

In religion and philosophy, the authority of the Orthodox Church was challenged. Many hearkened to the message of Vladimir Solov'iev, a mystical nationalist. His writings combined poetic playfulness and cynicism with moral earnestness and erotic spiritualism. Others followed the heretical teachings of Nietzsche. The common-sense assumptions of science and realism were replaced by a revival of idealism. By 1905 many intellectuals had abandoned the social reforms of the nineteenth century, and had turned to the goal of a spiritual revival, typically outside the Church. The Orthodox Church tried to respond to these influences by resurrecting the religious traditions of a unified and homogeneous old Russia. Unfortunately the Russia of 1900 was only partially Orthodox and not even remotely homogeneous. Religious revivalism failed to reunite the peoples of the Empire and contributed to the discontent of the minorities.

In art, Russians pioneered the explosions of expressionism, post-expressionism, and abstract art. Kandinsky, Malevich, Goncharova, Chagall and scores of other Russians, working at home and abroad, contributed to the radical undoing of the canons of art that had guided painters and sculptors since the Renaissance. Across the Western world the new art was denounced as decadent and revolting, and Russians played a major role in creating the furor. In music and dance this was the age of Benois, Stravinsky, Diaghilev, and of the *Ballet Russes*. Russian artists and performers shocked European audiences with primitive rhythms, elaborate stage sets, and fanciful costuming. In theater, Chekhov, along with Ibsen in Sweden and Shaw in Britain, pioneered modern drama. The well-made play of the nineteenth century gave way to daring forms and to new and controversial subject matter. Everywhere one looked, the old conventions were being challenged, and Russian high culture stood at the forefront of innovation.

Politically this was the age of the anarchists. Terrorists struck at Russian tsars, French, Italian, and American ministers and presidents. Not satisfied with reform in politics, the anarchists sought to eliminate politics and the state altogether. Russians, as usual, were among those who joined in this revolt against common sense and politics. When the editors of the famous eleventh edition of the Encyclopedia Britannica sought an authoritative voice to write an article on anarchism, they turned to a Russian, "PK," Peter Kropotkin, the "Anarchist Prince."

These were also the years, in Europe and in Russia, when society was rocked by the women's movement and the campaign for women's suffrage. In Russia, radical socialist writers and theoreticians, male and female, demanded equal access to education, the work-place, and the professions. At every level of society one heard calls for financial and personal independence for women and an end to the male domination of wealth and power. Early Russian feminists, along with their European counterparts, were fascinated by Frederick Engels' 1972 analysis in *The Origins of the Family, Private Property and the State*. Engels suggested that an inevitable future social revolution would restore women to an equality not known since primitive times. Many now speculated on the role of women and the family in the society of the future.

Ordinary Russians participated in these cultural revolutions through film, magazines and books. By 1914, major efforts by the central government, the Church, and the elective urban and rural governments had virtually eliminated Russia's notoriously high illiteracy rates in European Russia. This created a large new segment of society reached by the arts and new ideas. Many Russians, even before the end of censorship in 1905, had become avid readers. Russia was no longer an illiterate peasant country. It consumed an impressive number of new titles each year, and a distinct popular culture began to emerge.

Cultural Diversity and the Revolution of 1917

Many who engaged in these multi-faceted cultural revolutions held high hopes for the Bolshevik seizure of power in 1917. Poets, writers, filmmakers, and artists flocked to the propaganda agencies of the new regime, hoping to mobilize the masses on behalf of revolutionary dreams of a new life and a new society. Avant-garde architects dreamed of socialist housing. Futuristic urban planners began to re-conceptualize what a city might look like. Theorists of the women's movement began to barrage the new government with ideas to transform love, marriage, the family, the factory, the farm, and the home.

Alas, within a few years, most of these avant-garde hopes were dashed. Lenin's revolution was made in the name of the working class and the peasants; the avant-garde seemed to come from the middle classes. In the battles that followed the Revolution, these middle-class innovators lost out. Certainly the fantastic artistic innovations of the previous years did not appeal to the common man. The Bolsheviks found themselves engaged in a brutal and lengthy civil war. In this context, encouraging bizarre artistic projects or liberating women from the drudgery of marriage were very low priorities. At the end of the First World War and during the subsequent civil war, it took frantic efforts just to hold the empire together. Factions inside Lenin's victorious socialist camp demanded discipline and immediate attention. The new government was unwilling to risk further divisions by encouraging novel ideas. The result was a vast discrepancy between the lofty goals and aspirations of European socialists before the Great War, and the ugly realities of Russian life between 1918 and the rise of Stalin a decade later.

The View from the Present

What is our view of Russia's revolutions today? We see now that the tsar's social revolution was kept alive when the Bolsheviks eliminated not only the old nobility, but the middle class as well. The economic revolution was re-born in Stalin's Five-Year-Plans to re-industrialize the nation after a generation of war and revolutionary turmoil. The political revolution survived because the aristocratic rule of the tsarist regime never returned. Unfortunately, the democratic dreams of 1905 were also crushed. The only still-born revolution was the exuberant pre-war cultural revolution, its life cut short by the need to conform in authoritarian

(Independent Newspaper from Russia, Inc.)

These figures of a worker and a peasant, familiar to most Russians, stood on a massive monument in Moscow celebrating the economic accomplishments of the USSR. Here they have packed up their hammer and sickle, and are marching off to an uncertain future.

Soviet society. It was killed by censorship, by dictated norms of socialist realism in art, and by political correctness and caution. The cultural revolution was cut short by the rise of Stalinism and the power of the totalitarian Soviet state.

Russia's twentieth century is ending with equally dramatic revolutions. The Communist Party has been declared illegal and its property seized. The Orthodox Church has regained its buildings in the Kremlin, and the Patriarch endorses governmental decisions. Secret libraries and archives are daily thrown open to scholars. National questions are presented to the people in public referenda. The right to own land has been affirmed. Private enterprise is encouraged, and slowly state enterprises are becoming private companies. Economic activity that was criminal a few years ago is now encouraged. Unfortunately, crime is also on the rise.

Much of this contemporary revolution began with Mikhail Gorbachev. When his book *Perestroika* appeared in 1987, his name was already a household word in America. Scholars, historians, and some journalists insisted that he was sincere, that he truly represented genuine revolutionary changes in Soviet politics and life. At the height of the Cold War, many conservative politicians and the American public at large urged caution, suggesting that Gorbachev represented nothing more than a KGB plot to nudge us into letting down our guard. In the end, these conservatives were proven wrong and a new era of Russian-American relations was born.

For the peoples of Eastern Europe, in the Republics of the old Soviet Union, and around the world, *Perestroika* was significant as a signal of new thinking, restructuring and a new approach to government. Gorbachev, the head of the Communist Party, suggested in print that the Soviet empire would not be held together by force. For the peoples of Russia, his book signaled a fundamental change in the political, economic, social, and cultural policies of their government. It announced a commitment to fundamental democratic self-government by the people, at least on the local level. It questioned the assumptions of the centrally-directed, state-owned and managed economy. It criticized the network of

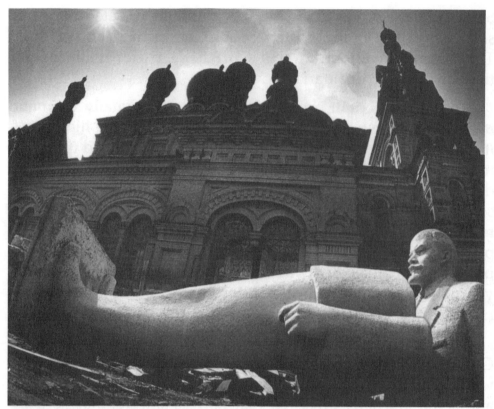

(Independent Newspaper from Russia, Inc.)

A broken idol. Gorbachev attempted to revitalize Lenin's role in the formation of the USSR. In his writings, he stressed Lenin's economic flexibility in creating the NEP, avoiding the dictatorial themes. That attempt failed. Here a dismantled statue of Lenin lays in front of a surviving Orthodox church.

socialist collective farms and industrial enterprises that dominated Soviet production. Socially it called for a new educational revolution that would root out stagnation, encourage creativity, and inspire people to participate in their nation's destiny. In short, Gorbachev's *Perestroika* announced revolutions as dramatic as those of 1917.

Gorbachev introduced the words *perestroika* or restructuring and *glasnost'* or openness into the English language. His policy of *glasnost'* was supposed to assure that his reforms survived. By announcing a policy of openness and by allowing public scrutiny of the government, abuses would be rooted out, and the power of old Soviet bureaucrats would be curbed. The policy of *glasnost'*, however, did not merely signify the accountability of officials. It also encouraged an unprecedented freedom of the press and of artistic expression. Gorbachev deplored the rigid policies of the Soviet past that had produced mass immigrations of intellectuals. He applauded the heated debates and dialogues inspired by *glasnost'* among new voluntary associations of filmmakers, writers, artists, composers, architects, theatrical figures, and journalists. He urged the intelligentsia to take charge of the nation's spiritual development. Gorbachev attempted to spark a new cultural revolution.

Gorbachev's national role may be ended. The Soviet Union he sought to reform on Leninist principles may be dismembered. But the freedom and the responsibility his policy of *glasnost'* placed on the Russian people have survived. With the loss of the Soviet empire, Russia has reemerged. But it is not the Russian Federation of the old Soviet Union. Just as the former national minorities now define themselves in terms of anti-Russianism, Russians are searching for their roots in the period before Soviet rule.

The printing presses of reemerging Russia are cranking out scores of books on the Romanovs and on Russia in the early

(AP/Wide World Photo)

Although recent public opinion polls indicate a general frustration with politics and politicians, demonstrators can be found for a wide array of solutions to Russia's problems. Here a woman outside the Kremlin's walls calls for the return of the tsars.

twentieth century. Art museums are arranging exhibitions of modernist works long denounced as decadent and relegated to musty cellars. Audiences are flocking to the cinema to see not only imported American films, but also the work of inventive and experimental new Russian filmmakers. Writings—fictional and non-fictional, poetic and journalistic—that would have tested the limits of censorship and invited deportation just a few years ago, are now hawked openly on the streets of Russian cities. The liturgy is again heard in Kremlin churches, and Russian Orthodox dignitaries bless political announcements. A journal of Russian women's writing has appeared. Political debate is intense. It includes the voices of democracy and liberalization, as well as the resurrected forces of reaction and anti-Semitism that greeted Russia's revolutions of the early twentieth century. While these nationalistic positions have ominous implications for the future of Russian democracy and legal order, they too are part of the search for identity that characterizes Russia today.

Suggested Readings

Conquest, Robert. *Stalin*. New York: Viking, 1990.

Conquest, Robert. *The Great Terror*. New York: Viking, 1990.

Daniels, Robert V. *Russia: Roots of Confrontation*. Cambridge, MA: Harvard University Press, 1985.

Gorbachev, Mikhail. *Perestroika*. New York: Harper & Row, 1987.

Lieven, Dominic. *Nicholas II*. New York: St. Martins, 1992.

Pipes, Richard. *Russia Under the Old Regime*. New York: Scribners, 1974.

Pipes, Richard. *The Russian Revolution*. New York: Vintage, 1990.

Riasanovsky, Nicholas. *A History of Russia*, 5th ed. Oxford: Oxford University Press, 1993.

Smith, Hedrick. *The New Russians*. New York: Random House, 1990.

Smith, Hedrick. *The Russians*. New York: Ballentine, 1984.

❧

The Russians at the Movies

Denise J. Youngblood

University of Vermont, Burlington, Vermont

For most of the last two centuries, Russians and Americans have led parallel lives, casting sidelong glances at each other, attracted and repelled at the same time. For many readers, this will be a surprising, and indeed, an unsettling proposition. Which two nations could be more unlike each other than the world's greatest democracy and the world's most awesome authoritarian regime? But the parallels are also remarkable. Both societies were neither here nor there: not European, not Asian—and proud of it. Both societies were slave societies, bearing the indelible scars of this tragic history late into the twentieth century. Both societies have been rocked to their foundations in modern times by brutal civil wars, the most destructive form of armed conflict. Both societies have been driven by "manifest destiny"—to the same Pacific Ocean—and deluded by visions of grandeur.

At one particular moment in time, however, after the Russian Revolution and Civil War of 1917–21, the comparison seems more than a bit farfetched. America, home territory for international capitalism, reeled against the astonishing propositions of Bolshevism to abolish private property, religion, traditional family values, and political freedom. Yet even in this most radical phase of the Russian Revolution, Russian and Americans could find common ground, in a not so improbable place: *at the movies.*

Revolution!

Americans understand revolution. One of our most cherished historical myths is that we are a revolutionary society. More Americans than we like to think were drawn to Russia by the romance of Revolution. The famous American reporter John Reed, buried in the Kremlin Wall, was but one, and his excitement was vividly captured in *Ten Days That Shook the World* , a book that was transformed into two memorable movies: Sergei Eisenstein's *October* and Warren Beatty's *Reds*. Americans enjoyed revolutionary Russia vicariously at their local movie theaters, watching numerous "fact-based" melodramas about decadent Russia in the last days of the empire. Greta Garbo in the film *Ninotchka* became our favorite "Russian."

But what about the Russians? While we were in the back row of the balcony watching Clara Bow, weren't they cheering at mass demonstrations, stringing up capitalists-in-effigy, singing bloodthirsty revolutionary songs? Some were, of course, but when the dust settled, Russians, too, could be found—at the movies. Throughout the Soviet period, and especially under Stalin, movies were a leading form of entertainment. After all, as Lenin said: *Cinema is for us the most important of the arts.*

The Roaring Twenties

At the age of only 23, Lev Kuleshov was one of Soviet cinema's leading directors and film theorists. He was also an American film buff. Kuleshov studied American movies endlessly, trying to determine the secret of their appeal: they had lots of action, a simple but compelling story, and a dash (or two, or three!) of love and sex. They had plenty of pretty people, wearing wonderful clothes, who were easily recognizable as either heroes or villains. In addition, and perhaps most important of all, they had a happy ending. As early as 1922, Kuleshov was able to offer this perceptive observation of the state of affairs:

Anyone who systematically frequents film theaters, viewing all the films that are released from Russian as well as foreign studios, anyone who has noticed which films cause the audience to react to cinematic action, would conclude the following: 1) foreign films appeal more than Russian ones; and 2) of the foreign films, all the American ones and detective stories appeal most.

Both superficial people and deep-thinking officials get equally frightened by 'Americanitis' and 'detectivitis' in the cinema and explain the success of particular films on the extraordinary decadence and poor tastes of the youth and the public of the third balcony. . . .[1]

At the time Kuleshov wrote these lines, Soviet society was just beginning to recover from the years of chaos and violence that had begun in August 1914 with World War I. The situation was bleak for film fans. Only sixteen Soviet films were produced in 1922, and worn-out copies of old German, French and a few American films were playing the theaters, along with leftovers of pre-revolutionary Russian cinema.

The New Economic Policy (NEP), introduced in 1921, quickly changed the situation. The NEP called for a mixed economy, allowing some private ownership. The success of the NEP overall is debatable, but in the film industry the results were astonishing. Although the industry remained the property of the state, it was self-financing. Studio heads had to turn a profit; therefore they had to make films people wanted to see. It was clear what that meant: audiences were sick of propaganda. So throughout the life of the NEP (until 1928), most of the budget of the state film trust went to the purchase of foreign films and production of Soviet films designed to appeal to European and American mass audiences.

As a result, a great many films shown in the USSR in the 1920s—an alarming 42 percent—were American "hits." Soviet films accounted for only 23 percent of the new titles, French and German films for the remaining 35 percent. By the end of the decade, the influence of American tastes, fashion, manner, and popular culture was considerable in major Soviet cities.

As impressive as these percentages were, they do not reveal the true extent of American domination at the box office. Most

Soviet films never played the "first-run" theaters in the cities, grand movie palaces that had been refurbished from the days of the empire. They had orchestras or jazz bands, snack bars, and high ticket prices. Instead, Soviet-produced films were sent, for the most part, to the film libraries of the trade union clubs. Workers who relied on the clubs for movie-going were furious at not getting the "latest" American pictures until the print was so worn out that they were often as much as one reel short.

American movies were heavily advertised, even in the Communist Party newspapers, and ran at least two to three months. *The Thief of Baghdad*, starring Douglas Fairbanks, was the biggest box office hit of the decade, and played Moscow's largest theatre, which seated over 1,000, for one year. The other two contenders for top box office honors of the 1920s were also American films: *The Mark of Zorro* and *The Sea Hawk*.

It is not surprising that the favorite movie stars were foreign as well. They were affectionately known to their adoring publics by their first names only—Charlie (Chaplin), Doug (Fairbanks), Mary (Pickford), and Conrad (Veidt). Only one, Harry Piel, a German star, was not well-known in the U.S.

The phenomenal popularity of Doug and Mary provides an excellent illustration of the state of Soviet film culture in the 1920s. Their faces appeared on the covers of Soviet film magazines. Their Soviet paperback biographies (published by a state-owned press) went through five reprintings in two years. The nearly quarter of a million copies sold exceeded the copies published on all Soviet actors combined. The July 1926 arrival of Doug and Mary in Moscow was greeted by screaming mobs of fans and recorded in Soviet newsreels for the movie theaters. It was also commemorated by one of the funniest Soviet films of the decade, Sergei Komarov's *Mary Pickford's Kiss* (1927). This film used cleverly edited footage from the Fairbanks/Pickford visit to make it appear that Doug and Mary were actually acting in the movie, with Mary seemingly planting a kiss on Goga, a star-struck movie usher played by the Soviet comedy sensation Igor Ilinsky, often known as the "Soviet Chaplin." As a result of Mary's kiss, Goga became an overnight sex symbol.

A few Soviet directors did, therefore, manage to produce films that made money at the box office. In virtually all cases, their movies were made in the "Western" style of *Mary Pickford's Kiss*. Lev Kuleshov, author of "Americanitis," himself serves as a prime example, directing a number of films that were creative take-offs on American movie genres. The most truly "American" of these was *The Extraordinary Adventures of Mr. West in the Land of the Bolsheviks* (1924), a zany satire about a naive American, the bespectacled president of the YMCA. Mr. West falls into the clutches of Soviet gangsters before being rescued by his trusty bodyguard, cowboy Jeddy, who brandishes a pair of six-shooters.

An even more popular example was *The Cigarette Girl from Mosselprom* (Yury Zhelyabuzhsky, 1924), which includes all the ingredients of "Americanism" in the movies. A pretty young girl is "discovered" and becomes a movie star. A rich American businessman falls in love with her, as does a handsome cameraman,

(Museum of Modern Art Film Stills Archive)

The naive American Mr. West, astonished by life in Soviet Russia in The Extraordinary Adventures of Mr. West in the Land of the Bolsheviks.

(Museum of Modern Art Film Stills Archive)

Love, Soviet-style: the typist, the clerk, and the cigarette girl together for the first time in The Cigarette Girl from Mosselprom.

and a bumbling clerk (also played by Igor Ilinsky). The romantic complications are many, the action is high-spirited, and everything turns out happily.

Many Bolsheviks were naturally worried about these movies. They feared that too many "Western bourgeois cultural values" would hopelessly corrupt Russians, ending their idealistic plans for creating a new society. Yet, although they expended much energy trying to fight this "cultural menace" in numerous articles in the 1920s, no amount of stuffy persuasion could turn Soviet audiences away from the foreign films they loved.

One figure helped ensure variety in movie-goers' film repertoire: Anatoly Lunacharsky, Commissar of Enlightenment (Secretary of Education and Culture, in our terminology). Although he was a long-time revolutionary, Lunacharsky was an influential fan and advocate of films. He was also married to the beautiful movie actress Natalya Rozenel, typecast as a "vamp." Lunacharsky wrote screenplays and a book about European filmmaking. He even appeared in several Soviet movies playing himself.

By 1928, however, ominous changes were afoot. That year marked the end of the New Economic Policy. In 1929, Lunacharsky resigned his post, in part to protest the new "hard line" in cultural policies. Stalin inaugurated a sweeping economic transformation of society known as the First Five-Year Plan, as well as a cultural revolution to end Western and "bourgeois" influences in Soviet culture. The state, in the midst of a massive industrialization campaign, couldn't afford to buy American movies. Furthermore, they couldn't allow "Americanism" to divert the public's attention from the enormous sacrifices that lay ahead.

Depressed? Escape!

By 1932, the cultural revolution had achieved its goals. The Soviet film industry was "independent." No foreign films were imported that year. Fewer than a dozen foreign films were shown publicly in the 1930s—compared to more than 1,700 in the preceding decade. Only one was an American film: Michael Curtiz's *Cabin in the Cotton*, a 1932 picture starring Bette Davis that showed how terrible life was in America. Soviet movie production was unable to fill the void since domestic production had declined by two-thirds.

The 1930s did not, however, completely end the influence of American films on Soviet cinema. Stalin was a passionate movie buff. He had a large screening room in his Kremlin apartments where he and his cronies continued to enjoy American pictures, especially musicals and "screwball" comedies. Stalin was, however, more than a spectator. He took an active interest in filmmaking. He terrified his favorite directors by calling in the middle of the night to discuss his ideas. He also made sure they saw the latest American movies, even if the public did not. After all, Stalin had called for life to become gayer, recognizing that Soviet citizens needed at least a momentary diversion from their hard lives.

The best example of this continued influence can be seen in the films of Grigory Alexandrov, whose musical comedies in the American style were popular favorites throughout the 1930s. The *Happy Guys* (1934), *Volga Volga* (1938), and The *Shining Path* (1940)

(*Museum of Modern Art Film Stills Archive*)

Lyubov Orlova, the Queen of the Soviet screen in the Stalin era, as American singer Marian Dixon in The Circus.

all reflect Alexandrov's familiarity with American movies. The most extraordinary example of continued "Americanism" in Soviet cinema is certainly Alexandrov's *The Circus* (1936).

The Circus features Lyubov Orlova, the only indisputable female movie star of the 1930s. Here Orlova plays a glamorous American singer named Marian Dixon. Marian has narrowly escaped being lynched in the U.S. for having a Negro lover and a mulatto child and arrives in the USSR as a circus performer under the "protection" of an unsavory, apparently German, fascist. She easily finds stardom and a chic apartment with an enormous, highly polished piano, but love eludes her as long as she remains in the fascist's foul clutches. The finale rivals any Hollywood production of the 1930s for glitter, grandeur, and pure schmaltz. Marian and her new lover, an ex-aviator turned circus performer, stage an extraordinary space-age fantasy while the multi-ethnic circus audience croons a lullaby to her child.

While it would be seriously misleading to paint too rosy a picture of Soviet filmmaking in the 1930s, films like *The Circus* were an essential part of the program. Also, we should remember that movies in the U.S. during the Great Depression (and during other difficult times) played a similar function in society—to distract people from their very real troubles. Romantic extravaganzas about beautiful people living their fairy-tale lives were preferable to reality in both countries. People could dream a few hours of their trouble-ridden lives away for a song and a smile at the movies.

Cold War and the Thaw

World War II provides few points of comparison, not surprising given the extent of the calamity that befell the Soviet Union: 20-27 million lives lost by war's end. One hundred percent of Soviet production during the war was directed to war films, a situation unparalleled in any other combatant nation. Most of these films had women as protagonists, reflecting the critical role women played defending their "motherland."

With the onset of the Cold War, however, parallels between Soviet and American movie-making once again became obvious. For every *Manchurian Candidate* on American screens during the Cold War, there was an equally chilling and "realistic" Soviet cinematic counterpart. But Soviet filmmakers turned away from Cold War themes more quickly than did Hollywood directors.

The movies came to life again during Khrushchev's cultural "Thaw" of the 1950s, with a series of touching and sentimental war pictures. One of the best was Mikhail Kalatozov's *The Cranes Are Flying*, a poignant look at the impact of the war on those who survived. The film industry slowly revived, but as good as some Soviet directors were, American movies still had a signature all their own, the more so for being forbidden fruit.

Importation of American films was so erratic in the thirty years following World War II that Soviet audiences saw Elizabeth Taylor as *Cleopatra* seventeen years late. Yet it was advertised lavishly in Moscow in 1979 as a "new American movie" and played the largest downtown theaters. Clearly, the hunger for contact with the outside world through the movies had not abated in six decades of Soviet power.

In fact, the only verifiable box office hit for a Soviet-made picture in the 1970s was Vladimir Menshov's 1979 *Moscow Does Not Believe in Tears*. This example is an instructive one. An obvious tribute to the Hollywood "girlfriend" films of the 1940s and 1950s, the movie follows three young women through the trials and tribulations of life. The heroine is Katia, spunky and attractive, who overcomes an out-of-wedlock pregnancy in order to find true love and become a factory manager. This unexceptional though charming movie done in the American-style drew Soviet audiences in droves—100 million tickets sold, making it the biggest box office smash in Soviet film history. Hollywood returned the compliment by awarding this rather old-fashioned movie the Oscar for Best Foreign Picture in 1980, only the second time a Soviet film has won the honor (Sergei Bondarchuk's epic adaptation of Tolstoy's *War and Peace* was the first some dozen years earlier).

(Museum of Modern Art Film Stills Archive)

Liudmila and Katia living it up in the professor's apartment in Moscow Does Not Believe In Tears.

Culture Clash

Given that the malaise in the film industry was obvious by the early 1980s, Gorbachev's accession to the post of Communist Party Secretary in 1985 was a cause for rejoicing among moviemakers. The Cinematographers' Union was one of Gorbachev's earliest and most important sources of support, and several filmmakers became prominent politicians. Previously censored films like Alexander Askoldov's *The Commissar* came "off the shelf" and won prizes at international film festivals.

Soviet cinema had to show a profit for the first time since the New Economic Policy ended sixty years earlier. Production money was once again channeled into making entertainment films that the public wanted to see. Artists could now write, paint, film, stage . . . anything they wanted. This new-found freedom led to an orgy of self-indulgence, focusing mainly on the most forbidden of all the forbidden fruits of the era of stagnation: erotica and Stalin—or best of all, some combination of the two. Shock value became the stock and trade of the film industry.

That was only the beginning. Elem Klimov, the head of the restructured Union of Cinematographers, and his erstwhile successor, Andrei Smirnov, entertained grand plans for transforming the Soviet film industry Hollywood style. They hoped to revive a scheme from the 1930s to establish a Paramount or Universal Studios-type tourist attraction on the shores of the Black Sea. The Moscow International Film Festival expanded. *Sovexportfilm,* the central export agency, jacked up its prices and took to publishing glossy catalogues in anticipation of a rush of hard currency buyers.

The excitement of these heady days increased with the release of a bona fide international hit: Vasily Pichul's *Little Vera* (1989). This movie is a depressing but provocative examination of poverty and alienation. However, it attracted audiences at home and abroad for other reasons: Natalya Negoda with her clothes on, Natalya Negoda with her clothes off, Natalya Negoda making love. This very same Natalya became the first Soviet citizen to present an Oscar in an Academy Awards ceremony—and to be featured in a *Playboy* magazine centerfold.

Despite these promising beginnings, the Soviet film industry fizzled even before the USSR came to an abrupt end in 1991. Among *glasnost'*-era films, only *Little Vera* received widespread distribution in the U.S. in the past decade. The acceptance of new domestic films has been little better in the Soviet/Russian market. Established Russian directors, who are accustomed to thinking of themselves as "artists," for the most part have had a terrible time adapting to market requirements. They don't know how to attract financing or audiences.

So a host of new names has come to the forefront. In the words of one Russian movie critic, Russian-made pictures these days tend to focus on:

> dark disillusionment, drug addiction and satanic rock music ... [with] characters [who] race around on motorcycles, cut each other with knives, take their own lives, and so forth.[2]

In other words, they are Soviet-made "American" movies, complete with American violence!

But who, it must be asked, makes American-style movies better than Americans? By April 1991, eight months before the final dissolution of the USSR, only 22 of the 313 films showing in Moscow were Soviet. The vast majority of these 291 foreign movies were American films, and they were being screened in the best and largest "first-run" theaters. Despite the fact that the American pictures Soviet audiences most wanted to see were the expensive hits from the major Hollywood studios, the titles being screened were films most Americans had never heard of (or would never admit to having heard of): *The Beach Girls, Hot Target, The Nine Deaths of the Ninja.* As a former director of *Sovexportfilm*, put it: "In point of fact, we aren't linking up with Western civilization, but with its trash. . . ."[3]

The present situation in the cinema of the former USSR is one of extreme confusion and demoralization. The painful realities of commercial "censorship" (meaning, the demands of catering to the market) are pervasive. Funding for movie-making has vanished, and Russian production of feature films is now at fewer than a dozen a year.

Furthermore, the globalization of world culture based on an American model does not make the future of a commercially viable Russian-language cinema look promising. Prominent directors like Andrei Konchalovsky have realized this and have turned to making English-language films on Russian themes for survival. A perfect example is Konchalovsky's 1991 movie *The Inner Circle*, a "true story" melodrama about Stalin's personal movie projectionist, featuring American and English actors like Tom Hulce and Bob Hoskins in the leading roles. It is an example that saddened struggling Russian filmmakers. They refused to accept as natural or inevitable the status of "vassals" of Hollywood. They found it impossibly painful to accept that Russian audiences, like mass audiences elsewhere, were in love with American movies.

As a result, a new "anti-Americanism" began to emerge several years ago in cultural circles. This phenomenon is becoming increasingly pronounced today. The manifesto of this cultural anti-Americanism in cinema appeared in the liberal newspaper *The Literary Gazette* in 1990. Critic Yury Gladilshchikov lamented:

> It's as if we're now in the same situation as Hollywood was when it was just starting to develop. We're like the Hollywood, say, of 1915, but . . . surrounded by cinematic superpowers. . . . Look at history and at present-day Europe. More than two years ago, a desperate letter from leading European talents appeared: European cinema is dying because of its inability to withstand the Americans' onslaught! . . . Are we ready for this?[4]

Gladilshchikov bitterly concluded that, while directors are not ready to witness the destruction of Russian cinema, ordinary Russian movie-goers are. Alas, the Russian audience prefers entertainment to art.

The New Cultural Battleground

As the political climate in the USSR and Eastern Europe rapidly changes in a way Westerners find palatable, there has been a corresponding surge of talk about "internationalization" and "globalization" of politics and culture. American scholar Francis Fukuyama has even claimed that history has "ended" in the

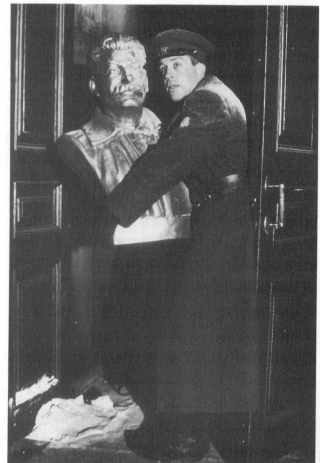

American actor Tom Hulce as the movie projectionist rescuing Stalin in the U.S./Soviet co-production The Inner Circle.

(Museum of Modern Art Film Stills Archive)

triumph of capitalism. At the same time, and partly in reaction to this, a resurgence of nationalism has swept Eastern Europe and Eurasia. This cultural arena promises to be a major battleground, perhaps for a new *Cultural Cold War* between Russians and Americans.

The "big business" of American mass media presents a formidable foe for the under-capitalized Russians. Our mass media are, in fact, quite conscious of their roles in this process of international cultural homogenization. The American Academy of Motion Picture Arts and Sciences made this abundantly clear in its 1990 Academy Awards presentation. This program emphasized the role of American movies in unifying the world. To emphasize the point, American actor Jack Lemmon and Soviet actress Natalya Negoda (*Little Vera*) were featured live, complete with audio glitches, from the Hotel Rossiya in Moscow. As one columnist quipped, it appeared that the Academy was promoting itself as the West Coast Division of the United Nations!

Russian filmmakers continue to dream that they can resist cinematic "Americanization." They dare to hope that they can create a new Russian movie industry in an Americanized world. But many difficult questions remain unanswered. What value should be placed on preserving national cultures? Should the freedom of choice—newly provided by the capitalist marketplace—be restricted, in order to protect Russian cinema? Or do the Russian people have the right to see whatever they want, in this case, American movies? This debate over the tensions between untrammeled liberty and traditional values is not unique to Russia. It is, in fact, one of the central paradoxes of our time.

Endnotes

[1] Ronald Levaco, ed. and trans., *Kuleshov on Film*. Berkeley, CA: 1974, pp. 127-30

[2] Yury Gladilshchikov, "America Gave Russia a Steamship," *Current Digest of the Soviet Press* 42, No. 31,1990, p. 12.

[3] Oleg Rudnev, "What Kind of Cinema Will Dr. Tagi-Zade Prescribe for Us?" *Current Digest of the Soviet Press* 43, No. 18, 1990, pp. 10-11.

[4] Gladilshchikov, "America Gave Russia a Steamship," p.13.

Suggested Reading

Horton, Andrew and Brashinsky, Michael. *The Zero Hour: Glasnost and Soviet Cinema in Transition*. Princeton: Princeton University Press, 1992.

Kenez, Peter. *Cinema and Soviet Society, 1917-1953*. Cambridge: Cambridge University Press, 1992.

Lawton, Anna, ed. *The Red Screen: Politics, Society, Art in Soviet Cinema*. London: Routledge, 1992.

Lawton, Anna. *Kinoglasnost: Soviet Cinema in Our Time*. Cambridge: Cambridge University Press, 1992.

Stites, Richard. *Russian Popular Culture: Entertainment and Society since 1900*. Cambridge: Cambridge University Press, 1992.

Youngblood, Denise J. *Movies for the Masses: Popular Cinema and Soviet Society In the 1920s.* Cambridge: Cambridge University Press, 1992.

Youngblood, Denise J. *Soviet Cinema in the Silent Era, 1918–1935.* Austin: University of Texas Press, 1991.

Zorkaya, Neya. *The Illustrated History of Soviet Cinema.* New York: Hippocrene Books, 1989.

ℭℨ

The Yellow Moon Has Met a Shadow:

Control and the Creative Voice in Early Soviet Literature

Irwin Weil

Northwestern University, Evanston, Illinois

Russia's twentieth century bears witness to the power of the three revolutions that took place between 1905 and 1917. John Reed, a perceptive American journalist, labeled the last revolution *Ten Days That Shook the World,* but altogether they overturned a political order which had ruled the vast tsarist Russian empire for over 300 years. They led to the development of a Marxist government which, by the 1930s, not only controlled politics and economics but was further determined to control the imagination and creativity of the Russian people. The Bolsheviks proclaimed that good Marxist writers would describe every human activity in conformity with communist doctrine. For three generations the Marxist Soviet government was obsessed with controlling and manipulating the Soviet official and popular culture in a direction it claimed to be scientifically socialist, and which it considered desirable for humankind.

Rebellion and Dogma: An Uneasy Coexistence

The Soviet Union came into existence at a time when Russian high culture, especially literature, was flourishing, largely in rebellion against nineteenth-century romanticism, realism, and especially "Civic Art" (art in the service of society). The most creative writers of Russia's Silver Age, from the 1890s to 1917, rejected the notions that art was dependent on political ideology or was meant to improve society. They valiantly endeavored to achieve the autonomy of art—the complete freedom of the writer to present the world as he or she saw it. In many cases, it seemed that the more fantastic and removed from everyday life, and even logic, the better these artists and critics liked such works. The Marxist revolutionaries and their "neo-realist" writers, on the contrary, considered such writing and art exaggerated, silly, and reactionary. The Twenties saw the uneasy coexistence of this extraordinarily colorful, creative, thoughtful, and insightful literary culture, and that of its socialist enemies.

To Stay or Not to Stay

When the Bolshevik government came to power, its policies created tremendous divisions within the culture of the Russian world. Many of the writers and intellectuals were eventually imprisoned or executed, or they joined the huge waves of emigrants from Red Russia. Large colonies of Russian émigré culture grew up in Berlin and Paris in the 1920s. Smaller ones existed in other European cities and later in America. Among those people were literally thousands of writers, intellectuals, and artists of all kinds.

For example, Vladimir Nabokov (1899–1977), one courageous émigré literary figure of this time, developed creative new paths in literature. His unique style of writing and criticism, together with scientific writing on butterflies, shook the imagination of the literary world. There have been many different reactions to his ideas and writing, but no one denies his integrity and talent. He expressed poignantly the complex reactions of a cultured, prerevolutionary Russian living in Europe, and later, in America. His 1958 novel *Lolita* has become one of the most important works describing a cultivated immigrant's reaction to American popular culture. Nabokov's European narrator's descriptions were unusual and evocative:

> The pink old fellow peered good-naturedly at Lo—still squatting, listening in profile, lips parted, to what the dog's mistress, an ancient lady swathed in violet veils, was telling her from the depths of a cretonne easy chair. [1]

The Revolution thus donated one of Russia's great gifts to American literature.

For those artists, writers, and intellectuals who stayed in the USSR or returned from emigration, the situation became very difficult. Those who refused to lend their efforts to a regime which they detested had few choices. They either moved to another line of work or perished.

Other artists and creators, of course, enthusiastically committed themselves to the movement which they believed would lead to true communism. They eagerly formed the propagandistic and artistic cadres of the new revolutionary government, including its campaign against the Church. They imagined communism as a nurturing system which would be the salvation of the world. Many were mediocre writers who survived only by joining the victorious Bolsheviks. They conjured up a new socialist culture which would be the product of an entirely *New Soviet Man* without fear, without exploitation, without bourgeois sicknesses. They could not foresee that such a creature would eventually be like a robot, all muscle and no creativity. They naively assumed that the past could be completely destroyed. Such people did enormous damage to the rich Russian tradition of ideas, churches, and icons.

Writers of the Revolution

Talented individuals could also be attracted to the Revolution. One great exception to the general mediocrity of artists faithful to the Communist Party was Vladimir Mayakovsky (1893–1930), poet, artist, and self-styled Revolutionary Tribune. He used language stirringly mixed with traditional church formulations, Marxist jargon, doggerel, and the passionate language of love and bravado. His rhythms deliberately flaunted the classical manner of Russian poetry, even in its printed form. With a dramatic embrace of contrasts and opposites, he swash-buckled his way through the literary and ideological life of the early Soviet Union. Toward the 1930s, however, both the government and he began to realize that such an independent stance could no longer be tolerated. His suicide by Russian roulette prevented an even more tragic fate which doubtless would have met him under Stalin's purges.

Mayakovsky eerily forecast such a fate in a play, *The Bedbug*. When the main character in the play wakes up after being frozen for fifty years, he discovers a strange new society. It is a parody on Mayakovsky's own communist ideals. The new society's rational scientists put the main character in a zoo cage, as a strange animal left over from earlier times. In a chilling address to the Moscow Art Theatre audience of 1930, he proclaims:

> Citizens! Brothers! My own people! Darlings! How did you get here? So many of you! When were you unfrozen? Why am I alone in the cage? Darlings, friends, come and join me! Why am I suffering? Citizens?
>
> The guests in the play reply: 'Oh how horrible. Professor put a stop to it! Ah, but don't shoot it!'
>
> The director says: 'Disperse quietly, citizens, until tomorrow. (Music) Let's have a march!'

This was very powerful writing for the people of Moscow who were about to undergo mass arrests.

The dead Mayakovsky, no longer a threat, was canonized by Stalin and subsequent Soviet leaders. Yet, the force of his talent, personality, and some of his poetry overcame this official lacquer. In a central Moscow square, his monument, called "Triumphal" is a magnificent representation of his sneering smile, his aspiring yet clumsy body and his unique aura. It may well represent the enormity of the present, post-Soviet struggle as Russia searches for its identity in the chaos of freedom.

Another writer who tried to support the Soviet government was a man with a considerable pre-revolutionary reputation. In fact, at the beginning of the 1900s, he was already an international celebrity. He called himself M. Gorky ("Bitter"), although his real name was Aleksei Peshkov (1868-1936). While quite capable of urging people to commit murderous acts—*If our opponent does not surrender, we will annihilate him!*—Gorky was also a writer with real mastery over the Russian language, its folk poetry, and religious traditions. He befriended the Russian revolutionaries abroad before 1917.

Unlike Mayakovsky, who eagerly joined the Revolution, when Gorky saw Lenin's and Trotsky's terrorism and intellectual repression, he vehemently protested for many months. When Lenin closed down his newspaper, Gorky created a new literatry series. Its goal was to popularize good literature from many cultures and languages. He also tried to save the lives of intellectuals who were condemned by the Soviet government by intervening with his old friend Lenin. This effort, however, was doomed to fail. Gorky, for example, tried to save the life of the condemned poet, Gumilev. Lenin promised to do so, and Gorky informed the family. Unfortunately, the order was lost, Gumilev was shot, and Gorky felt compromised. He left Russia in 1922 and lived abroad for several years. Gorky returned later in the 1920s, living under Stalin until 1936. Scholars still argue whether he was murdered. His death signaled the beginning of the mass purges, in which many people whom Gorky had protected perished. Among them were the literary critic Sviatopolk-Mirsky and the enormously popular Isaac Babel, author of stories about the Red Army.

After his death, Gorky's name was exploited by the regime in many ways. Every conceivable place was named after him, including

(Ardis Publishers, Our Age by Moses Nappelbaum, Ilya Rudiak, ed., 1984)

Maxim Gorky (1868–1936)

his native city, institutes, schools, and factories. As a result, his name became an object of ridicule among educated people, while his truly good works, both personal and literary, were de-emphasized. Nevertheless, Gorky had done what he could to popularize the best parts of Russian and world literary traditions, and he fought against those who worked to destroy them. Considerable debate now rages around his name. In many ways, his fate and reputation illustrate the dramatic twentieth-century struggles of Russian literature and culture.

Mayakovsky and Gorky were the most idealized of the writers with large reputations who tried to make peace with the new regime. But there were others, especially in the 1920s. Perhaps the most creative was a group called the "Serapion Brothers," named after a famous literary hermit from German literature. They urged each other to write independently, following no instructions except their own creative desires and feelings. Gorky himself was a political and literary protector of this group. Such independence became impossible by about 1930.

Difficult Times—Difficult Choices

In the 1930s the regime devised the official "Union of Soviet Writers," which soon controlled the direction and production of literature. Anyone who wanted to make a living through writing, or simply to be published officially, had to obtain his or her royalties and payments through this tightly controlled union. Once it was established, very few writers dared to defy the union. Those few who did were either extremely stealthy or practiced an almost mad kind of courage.

Still, considering censorship and the difficult circumstances of Soviet life, Russia produced an impressively large number of talented and productive people. Most of them tried to occupy a sort of middle ground in relation to the government. They had no wish to join what seemed suicidal open opposition. At the same time, they had a peculiarly Russian compulsion to speak the truth about the human soul, just as their great nineteenth-century predecessors had done. The young Leo Tolstoy (1828–1910) had written that *truth, only truth, was the hero whom he loved above all else.*

Tolstoy's courage and principles were a powerful standard for the good Soviet writers who attempted to make these words a reality.

Mikhail Bulgakov (1891–1940) is now one of the most powerful and perennially popular Russian writers. His popularity was strongly reestablished in 1965, twenty-five years after his death. Trained as a medical doctor just before the revolutions of 1917, he started his writing career with a novel entitled *The Country Doctor*. It was a brilliant and original description of the life of a young Russian medical graduate assigned to a typically backward but colorful Russian peasant village. In it a sensitive reader could already hear the voice of a potential titan of literature. In the early Soviet days, Bulgakov made clear his satirical intent. His barbs aimed at Lenin and the Soviet regime later caused the Soviet apparatus to make clear their disapproval. The fear under which he wrote is evoked in the title of the first chapter of his masterwork: *Never Speak to Strangers*. Bulgakov quickly saw that unless he could find some way of working which evaded Soviet censorship, he would not be published.

Mikkhail Bulgakov (1891–1940)

(Ardis Publishers, Our Age by Moses Nappelbaum, Ilya Rudiak, ed., 1984)

In the 1930s, a remarkable incident in Soviet literature occurred. Bulgakov wrote a letter to Stalin, which has been quoted repeatedly since Stalin's death in 1953. One could paraphrase it this way:

> I am facing starvation and oblivion, but don't expect me to change my old fashioned ideological convictions. Either let me go to Paris . . . or give me a job in the theatre, where I will direct and stage loyally, without a hint of opposition.

To many people's astonishment, the same Stalin whose apparatus butchered millions of people for supposed opposition, arranged a berth for Bulgakov in the Moscow Art Theatre. This was surprising, since many of these victims were far less openly opposed than Bulgakov's writing had been. But then, in many of Bulgakov's fictitious stories, a strong governmental hand often saved the protagonists. Perhaps life was following literature.

At this time the world-famous Stanislavsky was director of the Moscow Art Theatre. He and Bulgakov reacted to one another like oil and water. The result was one of the most comic and powerful parodies ever written on a great creative personality. Bulgakov's theatrical novel, sometimes known as *Black Snow*, battered Stanislavsky, his ideas, and his methods, all of which were revered throughout the theatrical world in Russia and in the West. In the novel, a writer is saved from suicide by a great theatre director's intervention. Overjoyed to see the possibility of his play being produced, the writer joyously comes to the theatre. To his dismay, he sees a series of foolish games being performed by actors which have nothing to do with the reality of his play. The result was both comic and tragic, a humiliating parody of Stanislavsky's famous "method-acting." As one might easily understand, this did not make Bulgakov's dramatic productions popular with Stanislavsky's followers at the Moscow Art Theatre.

Bulgakov wrote in increasing isolation. Just before his death in 1940, he finished one of the greatest novels of the twentieth century, *The Master and Margarita*. It was a re-telling, in different form, of Goethe's masterpiece, *Faust*, and of the book of Matthew in *The New Testament*. It was also a searing satire on Soviet culture, most especially on the Soviet Writers' Union and its servile creatures. The book would have been vaporized in Stalin's day, so Bulgakov's widow carefully hid it away. In Soviet parlance, it was "written for the desk drawer." About ten to twelve years after Stalin's death, in the 1960s, the widow dared to show it to a Soviet magazine, *Nov Mir* (New World), known in those days for its relative liberalism.

The resulting publication, even though some parts were cut out, shook the Soviet Republic and caught the attention of the literary world. It portrayed a courageous young woman magically flying around Moscow, shattering the windows in apartments of dishonest critics and bureaucrats.

> [Margarita] crossed the Arbat, rose higher, to the fourth floors, floated past the dazzling signs over the theater building on the corner and turned into a narrow lane bordered by tall buildings. All the windows were open and everywhere she heard the music of radios. Curious, Margarita peeked into one of the windows. She saw a kitchen. Two primuses roared on the stove; two women stood near them with spoons in their hands, quarreling.
>
> 'You should turn off the light in the bathroom when you leave, Pelageya Petrovna,' said the woman before a saucepan with some steaming food, 'or we'll apply for your eviction.'
>
> 'You're a fine one yourself,' answered the other.
>
> 'You're both fine ones,' Margarita said loudly, tumbling across the window sill into the kitchen.
>
> The quarreling women turned to the voice and froze with the dirty spoons in their hands. Margarita cautiously stretched out her hand between them, and turned out both primus stoves. The women gasped and opened their mouths. But Margarita was already bored in the kitchen and flew out into the lane.

The story also showed a bemused devil named Azazello who gave Margarita her magical power. His sarcastic comments about the new Soviet Moscow delighted those who had suffered from Soviet repression.[2]

> 'Ah, don't listen to the poor woman, Messire! The basement is long occupied by another man, and generally, things never return to what they were.' [The Master] pressed his cheek to his beloved's head, putting his arm around Margarita, and began to mutter: 'My poor dear, my poor dear.'
>
> 'They never do, you say?' said Woland. 'That is true. But we shall try.' And he called: 'Azazello!'
>
> At once a man dropped from the ceiling on the floor—distracted and almost beside himself, in nothing but underwear, but for some reason with a suitcase in his hands and in a cap. The man trembled and bobbed up and down with terror.
>
> 'Mogarych?' Azazello asked the citizen who had dropped down from the sky.
>
> 'Aloisy Mogarych,' he answered, quaking.
>
> 'Was it you who wrote a denunciation of this man after reading Latunsky's article about his novel?' asked Azazello.
>
> The citizen turned blue and burst into tears of repentance.

'You wanted to move into his rooms?' Azazello drawled as soul-fully as he could.

'I added a bathroom. . .' Mogarych cried, his teeth chattering. Then, in sheer terror, he began to rant utter nonsense: 'The whitewash alone . . . the vitriol. . . .

'You built a bathroom? That's good,' Azazello said approvingly. 'He has to take baths.' And he shouted: 'Out!'

Mogarych was turned upside down and swept out of Woland's bedroom through the open window. [3]

The novel caught the attention of Moscow's most creative theatre, the Taganka, and the theatrical adaptation of the novel became an integral part of the contemporary Soviet, then Russian cultural repertoire. Twenty to thirty years after his death, Bulgakov's name remained an inspiration for a new generation of Soviet and then Russian people. *The Master and Margarita* is a rare and acutely Russian story, conveying the ideas of resurrection and immortality so often present in traditional Russian literature. It in some ways parallels Fyodor Dostoevsky's (1821–81) classic novel, *The Brothers Karamazov* (1880), in which the brothers continue to thirst for immortality and eternity, despite evil works and actions. The endless struggle between good and evil is eloquently captured by Dostoyevsky's Ivan and Alyosha, as well as by Bulgakov's characters.

The Paradox of Repression

Such characters embody the paradox contained in Soviet history. This paradox is about a regime with a bloody and tyrannical aversion to truly great literature and ideas, but which unintentionally aided the publication and popularization of the very literature which it hated and feared. As Leo Tolstoy conveyed in *War and Peace, the real dynamics of history are far more complex than the ideas and powers of even the cleverest and most powerful of human beings.* In spite of its attempt to create a subservient and conformist literature, Soviet censorship indirectly created opponents who were boldly independent.

Concerts of Poets

Poetry in Russia spans high and popular culture. It was one of the most impressively developed genres of literature in old Russia and the USSR. Powerful and evocative language flowed out of men and women poets. Poetry was oriented toward past traditions in Russia and other parts of the world. For two to three generations, poetry was much more widely popular among the Soviet population than in other countries. In its printed form, and even more so in its oral form, poetry was a truly popular pastime and enterprise. The famous Poets' Days in Moscow and other cities attracted tens of thousands of spectators. What the Russians called concerts of poets attracted the same thousands of people we see at sports stadiums or rock concerts.

Among the scores of good poets were two outstanding men, Boris Pasternak (1890–1961) and Osip Mandelshtam ((1892–1938?), and two equally outstanding women, Anna Akhmatova (1888–1966) and Marina Tsvetaeva (1892–1941).

Pasternak originally prepared for a musical career before he discovered poetry, his real gift. His poetry deeply moved several generations of Russian language speakers, and the early regime was happy to use him as a literary ornament to send to Paris. He managed to stay alive during the purges of the 1930s, which claimed the lives of many first-rate intellectuals. At times he found refuge in translations, and his Russian versions of Shakespeare are superb. In his translations, the rhymes and passions of the Bard of

Boris Pasternak (1980–1961) with his family

(Ardis Publishers, Our Age by Moses Nappelbaum, Ilya Rudiak, ed., 1984)

Avon flow powerfully into the Slavic language. This was especially true of Shakespeare's songs, so moving in their sixteenth-century Elizabethan rhythms. Pasternak's musical heritage and early training help explain the charm of his rendition of Desdemona's *Willow Song* or Ophelia's *Song of St. Valentine's Day.*

Pasternak's poetry, his own and the works he translated, is a musical as well as literary rendition. His eloquent use of the Russian language reflected the richness of the language influenced in the early-nineteenth century by Pushkin (1799–1837). Pasternak's union of language and exalted feeling in matters both high and low made him a standard of Russian poetic taste and musicality.

Pasternak's first novel, *Dr. Zhivago,* was first considered, then rejected for publication by the Soviets. It then caused a great sensation when it was published in the West and earned Pasternak the Nobel Prize. This incident unleashed a vicious storm of invective against him in the official Soviet press. They called him a *pig who soiled his own nest.* The attacks only solidified his position among Russian readers. These same attacks undoubtedly generated the anxiety and tensions which hastened his death. His grave became a popular place of pilgrimage for the people who loved literature. The grave site was always cared for, in spite of Pasternak's political disfavor. The younger generation saw in him their link to Russia's great literary, poetic, and intellectual traditions. It is a shame that most American readers know him only as a novelist, and that the poems at the end of *Zhivago* have received so little attention by the public.

In the first poem at the end of *Dr. Zhivago,* Pasternak chose to represent the fate of Hamlet and Christ. They are entwined with the title character, Zhivago, and the difficulties of Soviet experience:

I cherish this, thy rigorous conception,
And I consent to play this part therein;
But another play is running at this moment,
So, for the present, release me from the cast.

And yet, the order of the acts has been schemed and plotted,
And nothing can avert the final curtain's fall.
I stand alone. All else is swamped by Pharisaism.
To live life to the end is not to cross a field.

A poet with an even more tragic end was Osip Mandelshtam. One of the most powerful raw talents for poetic language in the twentieth century, he touched readers as few poets ever have. For Russians, his poetry causes a physical reaction, similar to music which compels the listener to dance.

Two of Mandelshtam's lines were quoted by a Soviet scholar at the time of John Kennedy's assassination in 1963. At that time, Mandelshtam had not been published in the USSR for almost 35 years.

A man dies, and the heated sand cools down,
As yesterday's sun is carried out on a black stretcher.

He also wrote these words about the powerful Stalin (who was from Georgia, a country in the mountains, south of Russia):

One after another, his sentences hit like horseshoes!

He pounds them out. He always hits the nails, the balls.

After each death, he is like a Georgian tribesman,

Putting a raspberry in his mouth.

Mandelshtam fell out of favor with the terrorist police, originally called the Cheka, when he impulsively grabbed and destroyed a list of people scheduled to be executed. In the 1930s he was first exiled, then later, arrested and

Osip Mandelshtam (1892–1938)

(Ardis Publishers, Our Age by Moses Nappel-baum, Ilya Rudiak, ed., 1984)

placed in a camp where he perished under horrible conditions, perhaps first driven out of his mind.

Russian folklore and poetic lore are full of stories about Mandelshtam's last days and Stalin's phone call to Pasternak about his impending doom. Mandel-shtam's name became synonymous with Soviet literary martyrdom. His widow, Nadezhda, became an extraordinary heroine through her personal and literary faithfulness to the man and his poetry. She published two books of her own memoirs, never officially published in the pre-Gorbachev USSR, but widely known in Western Europe and America. In some ways, she created a place of pilgrimage akin to Pasternak's grave.

The poetry of Anna Akhmatova and Marina Tsvetaeva conveyed another voice in Soviet Russia. Akhmatova, a gifted poet and extraordinarily attractive young woman, became an outstanding heroine of Russian intellectual life in Soviet times. As a young woman, she was painted by Modigliani. Her family soon came under surveillance by the terrorist police, and her genuine poetic talent came to reveal those bureaucratic torturers all too well. One of her poems penetrated all of the USSR. In her *Requiem, Part II for Leningrad,* she deals with the grief of those caught in the mortal toils of the organization which self-righteously called itself the sword of the revolution.

(Ardis Publishers, Our Age by Moses Nappelbaum, Ilya Rudiak, ed., 1984)

Anna Akhmatova (1888–1966)

> *Quietly flows the quiet Don,*
> *Yellow moon slips into a home,*

He slips in with cap askew,
He sees a shadow, yellow moon,

This woman is ill,
This woman is alone,

Husband in the grave, son in prison,
Say a prayer for me. [4]

Akhmatova's poetry echoes with the strength, determination and emotion of a wounded woman and mother. Yet, it also has an over-arching intellectual power, capable of facing the human problems of her age—of any age.

Akhmatova was not arrested or physically maltreated. She became instead a prominent subject of the sleazy post-world War II attacks on the "disloyal" by Zhdanov, Stalin's censor and close associate. Zhdanov used a phrase about Akhmatova, which became a badge of honor for her and a stain of disgrace on Zhdanov's memory. He called her *half-nun, half-whore.* In the 1960s and early 1970s, Akhmatova became a kind of royal figure in the eyes of Soviet intellectuals. When she regally entered a noisy room, even those who feared contact with her for political and career reasons became silent and hung on her every word. Most of her publication was in the West, although Gorbachev's regime and subsequent events finally allowed her wide publication in Russia.

Marina Tsvetaeva experienced perhaps the most poignant tragedy in Soviet poetic experience. A gifted poet, her work grips the heart almost immediately. She emigrated and established a life for herself in Western Europe in the 1920s. In 1939, she decided to return to the Soviet Union. This was not an easy decision, as she reveals in her own poetry:

Can one return
To the home that's razed? . . .
That Russia where my youth
Is on the coins
Has gone.
Neither am I the same. [5]

Not long after her return to her homeland, Tsvetaeva was exiled to the provinces where she was forced to work as a washerwoman. Many of her family members were eliminated. Tsvetaeva's nerves did not hold out, and she hanged herself. She has become the Russian symbol of the poetic voice, weeping over the cruel fate of the intellectual and artistic people in Soviet Russia.

Out of the Shadows, Into the Light

Tsvetaeva's fate, like those of many other talented Soviet writers, illustrates the belief that the Revolutionary government ate up and destroyed its best writers. Yet even in the context of censorship and repression, many Soviet writers fought to preserve artistic and humane values. Through their efforts, they bore witness to the noblest side of human nature, both in Russia and in all of humanity. One weeps for their sacrifices and their suffering and takes pride in their remarkable achievements, now being rediscovered in reemerging Russia. The truth of early Soviet literature can now move out of the shadow, into the light.

Endnotes

[1] Nabokov, Vladimir. *Lolita.*

[2] Mikhail Bulgakov, *The Master and Margarita*, p. 255.

[3] Ibid., p. 301.

[4] Akhmatova, Anna. *The Complete Poems*, 2nd ed. Boston: Zephyr Press, 1992.

[5] Victoria Schweitzer, *Tsvetaeva*, p. 348.

Suggested Reading

Akhmatova, Anna. *The Complete Poems*, 2nd ed. Boston: Zephyr Press, 1992.

Brown, Clarence, editor. *The Portable Twentieth Century Russian Reader*. New York: Penguin, 1985.

Bulgakov, Mikhail. *Master and Margarita*. New York: Harper & Row, 1967.

Carlisle, Olga, editor. *Poets on Street Corners*. New York: Random House, 1968.

Dostoyevsky, Fyodor. *The Brothers Karamazov*. New York: Dell Publishing, 1956.

Gorky, M. *The Collected Short Stories*. New Jersey: Citadel Press, 1988.

Mandelshtam, Osip. *Poems from Mandelshtam*. New Jersey: Fairleigh Dickinson University Press, 1990.

Mayakovsky, Vladimir. *The Bedbug*. New York: World Publishing, 1970.

Nabokov, Vladimir. *Lolita*. New York: Knopf, 1992.

Pasternak, Boris. *Dr. Zhivago*. New York: Pantheon, 1958.

Schweitzer, Victoria. *Tsvetaeva*. New York: Ferrar, Straus & Giroux, 1993.

℘

The Shadow of a Dragonfly:
Dreams and Despair in Contemporary Russian Literature

Anatoly Vishevsky

Grinnell College, Grinnell, Iowa

The Thaw: Camp Literature and Young Prose

Shortly after Stalin's death in 1953, a liberalization took place in political and cultural life in the Soviet Union. The period was called the "thaw" after a novel of the same name by Ilia Ehrenburg. In the novel, the relaxing of internal policies after the death of Stalin was compared to the spring revival of nature that follows a severe winter.

One result of the thaw was the appearance of a number of works that dealt with Stalin's purges that took the lives of millions of innocent people. The horrifying truth brought forth powerful works of literature. This literature announced that people cannot hope for a better tomorrow unless they first understand the haunting darkness of yesterday. Writers tried to comprehend how the horrors of Stalin's times were possible and what made people go along with the atrocities.

In perhaps the most famous literary work dealing with this theme, *One Day in the Life of Ivan Denisovich*, Alexander Solzhenitsyn shows how a person wrongly convicted of a crime tries to preserve his decency and human identity in the inhuman conditions of a Gulag camp. The novella is an assertion of the strength of the human spirit, and a belief in its final victory over dark forces. Another writer of the "camp literature"—Varlam Shalamov, like Solzhenitsyn a former prisoner—paints a much gloomier picture in his collection *Kolyma Stories*. These stories, usually two to five pages long, are accounts of everyday life in the camp's mundane reality. The reality was that horrible murders were as routine as eating or sleeping. These stories are a testament to the knowledge that the laws of survival are cruel.

A different picture of the camps is seen in Georgi Vladimov's *Faithful Ruslan*. This story is told from the viewpoint of a guard dog that finds itself useless and "unemployed" after the prisoners have been released following the collapse of Stalin's system. Seeing the familiar human relationships through the dog's eyes enhances and dramatizes the readers' perception of the prison camp, the new angle allowing them to look at things from a new perspective.

One of the best poems to capture the atmosphere of the Stalinist era is Anna Akhmatova's "Requiem" taken here from *Selected Poems*, p. 146.

> *Stars of death stood above us, and Russia,*
> *In her innocence, twisted in pain*
> *Under blood-spattered boots, and the shudder*
> *Of the Black Marias in their train.*

In the poem, the poet waits in line with thousands of other Russian mothers, wives, and sisters. She does not know if today will be the day when her humble food parcel is rejected—which will mean the death of her loved one.

> *I've learned how faces droop and then grow hollow,*
> *How fear looks out from underneath the lids,*
> *How cheeks, carved out of suffering and of sorrow,*
> *Take on the lines of rough cuneiform scripts.*

How heads of curls, but lately black or ashen,
Turn suddenly to silver overnight,
Smiles fade on lips reduced to dread submission,
A hoarse dry laugh stands in for trembling fright.
I pray, not for myself alone, my cry
Goes up for all those with me there—for all. . .

A woman who anticipates hearing a sentence of death for her innocent son, Akhmatova becomes the voice of all mothers, and in the poem, draws a parallel to Mary, mother of Christ. By making this episode from her life and the life of her country the subject of the narrative poem, the poet judges the real "enemies of the people" and passes sentence on the executioners.

Another result of the thaw was the literary movement of the 1950s and early 1960s called "Young Prose." Young writers grouped around a new journal *Iunost'* (Youth), founded in 1955 by Valentin Kataev. They turned to new themes, to new horizons in life which opened up for the young with the death of Stalin and the fall of Stalinism. This literature was by young people for young people. The writers did not give their readers ideological lessons or teach them how to live, but rather, they expressed their own hopes and dreams for a new life. In literature, as in Soviet life after 1953, there existed an atmosphere of relative openness for the expression of ideas. As long as it did not jeopardize party doctrine, the state tolerated non-propagandistic, non-ideological literature. These young writers wrote about their student years, their first jobs, the joy and the sadness of characters who were, like their readers, just starting their lives. But above all, they voiced their dreams and hopes for a better life.

In his fantastic novella *The Steel Bird*, Vassily Aksyonov tells a story of victory over the forces of evil, represented by Popenkov, a steel creature, half-man, half-bird, reminiscent of *Zmei Gorynych*, a fire-dragon from old Russian fairy tales. Aksyonov uses this character to symbolize both Stalinism and fascism. The creature appears in a large apartment house in Moscow carrying two dripping shopping bags, one with meat and the other one with fish. Popenkov soon overtakes the whole house establishing himself physically, sexually, and ideologically as head of the community. The tenants of the house finally rebel, and the creature flies away, shouting something in its half-bird, half-human language, leaving a trail of black smoke. The tenement collapses, and its inhabitants move to a new building and a new life. This optimistic ending is marred by the fact that the steel bird is still lurking somewhere in the darkness waiting for the first opportunity to return.

Vassily Aksyonov (1932–   )

(Credit © Tom Wolff)

The Brezhnev Era: The Age of Irony

By the late 1960s the Young Prose movement had died out. The optimistic outlook of these young writers was based on the hope for social and cultural reform and for the return of the still-cherished values and ideals of the early post-revolutionary years. The movement's deterioration signaled the devaluation of those ideals and values. Just as Brezhnev's USSR was marked by stagnation, the dominant world view of Soviet writers in the late 1960s and 1970s turned to irony. This ironic mood was the result of the collapse of dreams and hopes for a better and freer society which had seemed possible during the temporary liberalization in the country's political atmosphere after Stalin's death. By this time, the ideals of the late 1950s no longer seemed valid. Most Soviet authors finally abandoned the belief that it was possible to change society. The brief thaw after Stalin's death ended. A new epoch began. This new epoch was characterized by the strengthening of the bureaucratic apparatus, by a dull and uneventful routine in art and everyday life, by disillusionment and despair. Since society could not be changed, the interest of writers shifted to the inner world of man. The new literary subject was not a

"Soviet citizen," but rather a generalized portrayal of an Earth inhabitant, detached and without real power.

In their imaginary world, these heroes could live and be happy, but any attempt to affirm themselves in the real world was bound to fail. These heroes were idealists. They looked for beauty and goodness in life, for the ideal love of a woman, for an ideal relationship between people. Their tragedy was that even their most modest dreams remained unfulfilled and unattainable. In the real world, these were individuals who craved to be heard, recognized, and acknowledged, but instead were constantly confronted with insensitivity, indifference, suspicion, and a denial of the goodness of human nature. All this causes them, as well as the reader, to sense the futility of life and the dullness of reality. The writers of this literature recognized the cruel irony and sympathized with their characters. They did not blame their characters for failing; they did not judge them. They attributed their heroes' inadequacies to the human predicament everywhere.

This ironic world-view is best illustrated by the works of two people who have become national heroes in Russia: Vladimir Vysotski, poet, song-writer, and bard; and Vasili Shukshin, a writer and film director. Vysotski's view of man is complex. In "Mangustos" he tells how people destroyed animals called mangustos because they were devouring all the vipers. According to Vysotski, people cannot live without venom and hence without snakes, because they really do not want to get rid of evil. Similar imagery can be found in his "Case History", in which the snake is the Biblical serpent and its venom represents forbidden knowledge. This author sees the history of mankind as the futile medical history of a person who is incurably ill.

Even dreams and fairy tales were ruined by the age of irony. Vysotski's song "There Is No More Lukomor'e" is a bitterly ironic account of the fate of Pushkin's fairy-tale land in modern times. In his long fairy tale in verse "Ruslan and Liudmila," written at the beginning of the 19th century, the Russian national poet Alexander Pushkin had drawn a picture of a fairy land that was familiar to every Russian child: a place where the river flows into the sea, and an oak, and a fairy-tale telling cat who is tied to the

(Photo courtesy of Ardis Publishers, Ann Arbor, Michigan)

Vasily Shukshin (1929–1974)

(Photo courtesy of V. Frumkin)

Vladimir Vysotski (1938–1980)

oak by a golden chain. Other wondrous creatures dwell in the picture: the wood spirit and the mermaid, a forest hut on chicken legs, thirty-three great warriors with their leader emerging from the sea, a sorcerer flying in the sky while fighting a mighty hero (bogatyr), an imprisoned tsar's daughter and her faithful wolf, a mortar which bears Baba-Iaga (a Russian fairy-tale witch), and the evil Koshchei Bessmertnyi (the Deathless) guarding his piles of gold.

Using the imagery of the fairy-tale world created by Pushkin, Vysotski constructs his own anti-fairy tale in which the wondrous image perishes as it is transformed by the new realities of bureaucracy, moral failure, corruption, and greed.

> *There is no more Lukomor'e, and there is no trace of oaks left,*
> *And even though the oaks are good for hardwood floors,*
> *The big guys who came out of their hut*
> *Have cut the oaks and used them for coffins.*

Vysotski's song continues as the house on chicken legs is burned, thirty-three fairy-tale warriors are raising chickens, the learned cat has turned his golden chain into money and is dictating his memoirs, the mermaid has borne a child out of wedlock and none of the thirty three warriors wants to take responsibility for the child, the wood spirit regularly gets drunk and beats his wife, all the wondrous creatures have been killed by hunters, and the sorcerer Chernomor finally abducts Liudmila. Evil prevails in this fairy-tale land, and this is just the beginning, says the author:

> *Oh, subside my grief*
> *In my heart,*
> *This is just an introduction*
> *And the fairy tale is yet to come.*

The fairy tale doesn't exist anymore. Its end is a metaphor for the collapse of traditional Russian values and the old way of life.

More recently, this theme was repeated in the works of the "village prose" writers. A desire to replace the unreliable communist doctrine with traditional moral values inspired a number of talented authors to revisit the old patriarchal Russian village. What they found was that even in the East, far removed from

У лукоморья дуб зеленый;
Златая цепь на дубе том:
И днем и ночью кот ученый
Все ходит по цепи кругом;
Идет направо — песнь заводит,
Налево — сказку говорит.

Там чудеса: там леший бродит,
Русалка на ветвях сидит;
Там на неведомых дорожках
Следы невиданных зверей;
Избушка там на курьих ножках
Стоит без окон, без дверей;

Alexander Pushkin's fairy tale world is captured in this wonderful illustration of an imaginary land that was familiar to every Russian child.

(from Fairy Tales by Pushkin, illustrated by B.N. Kukuliev and K.B. Kukulieva)

In this contemporary illustration by artist Eric Pervoukhin (1994) Pushkin's fairy tale world is transformed. The wondrous image has become a metaphor for the collapse of traditional Russian values and the old way of life.

Moscow, the ideal village was dying, having already been subjected to the destructive influence of the city.

In *Farewell to Matyora*, a novel by the Siberian writer Valentin Rasputin, the metaphoric death of the village is told using the real-life destruction of the island-village Matyora on the Angara River. The island and the village were buried at the bottom of a new reservoir as a result of the construction of a massive hydroelectric power station. But the real destruction of the village had begun even earlier, as its young inhabitants left home looking for a more exciting life in the city. Rasputin's novel centers on three generations of Matyora inhabitants and their different perspectives on the Soviet experience. The writer's anger and resentment are shown as he portrays the encroaching civilization that destroys peoples' homes, the graves of their ancestors, their memories, and their traditions. At the end of the novel, a fairy-tale creature, known as the Master of the Island, dies together with his island and the village of Matyora, as if symbolically bringing to an end any future hope for a magical solution. The fairy tales vanish with the world that created them, and with the end of the fairy tale, dreams also vanish from the world.

Dreams seem, at best, short-lived in Shukshin's story "Microscope." One day Andrei Erin, a carpenter, brings home a microscope that he claims he had received as a prize for his shock labor. The microscope changes Andrei's life drastically. He stops drinking and spends all his evenings at home, observing a fascinating new world on the other side of the lens. The hero's "discoveries" in the micro-world and his naive interpretation of the phenomena are funny and touching, yet the reader respects Andrei's devotion and thirst for knowledge. The hero's goals are also honorable—he dreams of freeing mankind from microbes and bacteria, and thus prolonging human life to one hundred and fifty years. The microscope is not a toy for Andrei, but rather an opportunity to prove that life is not in vain. The reader knows, though, that this attempt to escape reality is doomed and that the dream will be shattered. Even if a drunken friend had not accidentally revealed to Andrei's wife his secret (the microscope was bought with money that the hero claimed to have lost), the ending would be the same. Andrei himself accepts this stroke of destiny with surprising passivity, as if he expected it. Life assumes its normal path. Andrei goes back to drinking. He does not even try to stop his wife from returning the microscope, because he understands that the money is needed to buy coats for the children. "Real life" always hovers in the back of Andrei's mind. From the very beginning we know his protest is only a momentary escape and not a successful breakout.

The same is true for Vasili Atiasov from Evgeni Gushchin's "Shadow of a Dragonfly." This young carpenter's dream is no less incredible than those of Shukshin's heroes: he decides to build and fly his own helicopter. The dream appears suddenly, like a disease, and the only escape is to live it out. Neither the probable breakup of his marriage nor the scowling of his fellow-villagers distracts Vasili from his task. His wife, Varya, worries about him and seeks advice from the village palm-reader, who tells her: *Every man has some kind of a safety-valve. He either drinks or tells wild stories, or sometimes, like yours, builds some kind of trash, wasting himself.*

"Shadow of a Dragonfly" is the name the palm-reader gives to Vasili's disease. The helicopter built by the young carpenter becomes the manifestation of this name. Made of plywood, small, light, and fragile, the machine is the dream-symbol in the story. In contrast, a log house built by Vasili for his family stands for material values. This huge, shining, new home with carvings of kissing doves on the shutters is destined to win out over a fragile dream-helicopter made from a junkyard's odds and ends. The "Dragonfly" takes off but cannot climb high enough. It crashes into the trees. The description of the scene with the pine trees glowing in the sun and the "wall of the forest" brings back the image of the sturdy, lacquered log house. The story ends with the delayed arrival of winter. In the words of the author, *something had shifted in the customary flow of the seasons.* The character's actions are shown to be part of the natural pattern in which an occasional loss of rhythm is as essential as the regularity of nature's cycles. Vasili's dream is buried in the ruins of his plywood helicopter. He returns to his usual routine. Another hero's attempted escape from the world has failed.

Another form of escape, probably the most frequent in Russian literature (and daily life), is drinking. Evgeni Popov's story "Why Was There Shashko?" begins with the protagonist stating that he has been cured of alcoholism. A detailed account follows of the slaughter of Shashko, a little devil, that the lead

Evgeny Popov (1946–)

character finds in his apartment. At the end, the reader learns that the entire story takes place in an alcoholic daze where coldness, sobriety, and a corduroy sport coat are symbolic of the real world. But the nightmarish quality remains even after the character is cured, painfully reminding that an escape into the world of dreams is impossible.

> Answer me, why did I see Shashko, when as a matter of fact he never was and never could have been? Tell me, why is the real world more unreal than the unreal one and why are the faces of people in the street seized with meaningful horror and meaningless joy? Explain it to me, do Gogol, Hitler, Breugel, Hoffmann, Swift, and Stalin exist?

In "A Plane for Cologne," another of Popov's stories, an insignificant incident triggers trouble in a provincial town. At the bottom of the town's hierarchical ladder is an ageless cleaning woman named Glafira, whose failure to shovel the snow has caused the accident that kept a city official from reaching the airport to greet the leader of a friendly African nation. Crying, Glafira tells her superior the reason she was late for work: the day before, Glafira and her husband went to a county fair where they drank wine and ate shish-kebobs. Toward morning Glafira's husband got turned on and they started having sex. But he was so excited that he could not come for a long time, and when her husband and she finally reached an orgasm—an occasion so rare in Glafira's life that it acquires a festive aura—Glafira was already late for work. Glafira's story is so outrageous yet sincere that it touches even the woman's supervisor, a petty Stalinist bureaucrat. In such works, the dull and monotonous life of the characters is reduced to a mechanical existence, and is even more poignant because the mechanization of life in the society Popov depicts is real.

The dead end revealed by ironic writers in the 1960s and 1970s brought into the open a spreading mood of frustration and pessimism. A sense of doom descended on the Soviet Union. What started at the end of the 1960s as an intellectual, skeptical view of the human predicament, had by the beginning of the 1980s become a perspective common to the whole country: *continuing to lead the same life was impossible.* This feeling permeated all layers of society, even its top. This mood of despair helped to bring down the Communist Party and its system of government and ultimately led to the disintegration of the Soviet Union.

Russian Literature Today

The literature appearing today takes two main forms: historical fiction and the so-called "alternative literature." The first satisfies the growing desire for a national identity, a reevaluation of history from viewpoints contrary to Communist propaganda. This literature is not necessarily the result of the nationalist political movement but, as a rule, is in sympathy with it. "Alternative literature," on the other hand, is a loose term under which new forms of expression and new avenues in literature are grouped. A characteristic of the alternative writers is their break from anything associated with previous literature, not just official literature, but also the psychological realism that evolved after the death of Stalin. Their works often parody the ideas and forms of expression characteristic of the Soviet period. They debunk not only Soviet ideology, but ideological literature in general. This is a literature of destruction, aimed at annihilating its enemies and predecessors. It does not create anything new but rather is a parasite feeding off the body it is gradually destroying. The following poem by Irtenev is an example of such parodic literature:

Edible

Masha was eating porridge
Mama was eating Masha
Papa was eating Mama.
Grandma was eating turnip
Grandpa was devouring grandma
Until his stomach started hurting.
It's great to live in this world.
Louder with your song, kids!
Wider with your circle, kids!
What do we need the porridge for
On our planet,
When we have a friend nearby?

This seemingly simple rhyme contains complex imagery and a number of allusions. One allusion is to a fairy tale about a giant turnip that grew in a vegetable garden. In this old tale neither grandpa alone, nor grandpa and grandma who was helping by pulling the grandpa from behind, could pull the turnip out of the ground. Only with the help of the whole household, including the dog, the cat, and the mouse was the task achieved. The fairy tale illustrates the well-known motto "United we stand, divided we fall." The Russian verb "to eat" also means "to nag, to be on someone's case" and "to plot to have someone removed from a position of power." The parody is even more deliberate, in that the first line of the poem is the first sentence every Russian schoolchild reads (in *Bukvar*—the first primer or ABC book), and the last several lines are taken almost verbatim from a marching rhyme for Communist Young Pioneers.

Poetic form provides a fertile ground for the parody of socialist realism, and such parody is also prominent in contemporary Russian prose. A number of stories by Vladimir Sorokin are written with the specific goal of shocking readers, of making them reevaluate their attitude to the familiar in literature. In his stories Sorokin uses typical styles and themes from the literature of the Soviet period. The story "The Opening of the Season," for example, is written in the style of "village prose." The story depicts an ordinary hunting trip. The hunter, who is a city dweller and probably an important official, is being guided by a local peasant. The peasant idiom with its dialect and the slow-moving narrative are reminiscent of hundreds of similar stories. Their conversation deals with the deterioration of the villages, the corrupt influence of the city on the patriarchal life, the life of the forest and the habits of its creatures. The description of the hunt continues in the same peasant idiom, except the reader soon learns that a man has been substituted for a deer. Hunting for a man adds symbolic impact to the story. It is significant that the hunted man was lured to his death by a recording of songs by Vysotski. When the two hunters bend over their dead prey ready to cut out his heart and liver, the tape-recorder in the tree sings the words of the refrain from the song about Lukomor'e: *This is just an introduction, and the fairy tale is yet to come.*

Sorokin's "Passing Through" is written in the manner of the "official" writer and deals with another familiar theme in Soviet literature: the arrival of a high regional Party official at a District Party office. The story proceeds in the usual way: local leaders look for advice and wisdom from their superior and, as expected, are given both. The conversation centers on important agricultural topics and the plans for "propaganda and agitation of the masses" in the district. At the end of the visit the dignitary is shown an album that records the achievements of an important district factory. He looks through it attentively, and then suddenly climbs on the table, pulls down his trousers, and defecates on the open album. In the attempt to save the album, a district official stretches his hands to prevent the excrement from reaching the pages. The regional official then says good-bye and leaves as if nothing had happened, his offensive action a declaration of complete indifference.

The repulsiveness of this episode represents another development in contemporary Russian literature: this is the appearance of detailed descriptions of biological functions, the explicit portrayal of every conceivable sexual act, and scenes of violence that far outdo the Marquis de Sade's works in their goriness. Meant to express artistically the degeneration and deterioration of moral and ethical values—the inheritance received by the present generation from the Communist state—these stories abound in complex imagery. Necrophilia and the devouring of people during a sexual act are just two examples from the works of Victor Erofeev. Dreams have turned into nightmares, and the heroes have acquired hellish qualities.

It is such a picture that Popov draws in his story "Celebrated Encounters." A young man is on the way to see his girlfriend when he meets a famous writer in the elevator. The writer represents the establishment hated by the young man, and when the elevator becomes stuck, the two begin to fight. A number of details in the story allude to the fight between the fairy-tale forces of good and evil: the young men in the writer's entourage are called "little snakes," and certain phrases evoke the fairy tale killing of Koshchei the Deathless. The fight ends in a draw, but the young man proclaims his victory, since after the encounter the old man dies.

> I fought the old man and almost won the battle. And maybe I have won it. I am alive and independent, and he is dead. I wrote poetry dedicated to his memory. Would you like to hear it?

The story then twists with irony, as the young man loses his girlfriend, his fairy-tale princess, as the result of the fight. Popov adds another twist when, although the old man (Koshchei the Deathless) dies, the young man writes poetry about him and thus makes him immortal.

In the highly allegorical story "Seraphim" by Tatiana Tolstaia, the evil fairy-tale character appears as a fallen angel who can think of nothing but flying back into the sky. Everything on earth—men, children, and especially women, whom he sees as wicked and sinful—irritates the character. Earthly smells repel him and he wants to get away from people. Seraphim is particularly annoyed by a puppy that constantly follows him, trying to be friendly. Exasperated, the hero finally kills the dog. Then he feels claws growing in place of his fingers, and his face and body begin to be transformed. He then hears children calling him Zmei Gorynych—the frightful "Fire Dragon" from Russian folklore.

In one well-known Russian fairy tale a hero is sent on a quest: "Go I don't know where, and fetch I don't know what." In olden times, the fairy-tale hero could fulfill his task and bring the story to a happy ending. A similar task is given to the characters of contemporary Russian literature, but their qualities are far from heroic. The uncertainty in the country's future and the feeling of an approaching apocalypse translate in literature into macabre, surrealist, and absurd stories where heroes turn into villains. Yet, like Vasili and his "Shadow of a Dragonfly" dream, some things must be lived out. Hope against hope, perhaps the next "Dragonfly" will fly high enough to escape the mundane and the chaotic, and therein, create a new vision and attainable dreams.

Suggested Reading

Akhmatova, Anna. *Requiem and Poem without a Hero*, D. M. Thomas, tr. Athens: Ohio University Press, 1976.

Akhmatova, Anna. *Selected Poems*, Walter Arndt, Robin Campbell, and Carl R. Proffer, tr. Ann Arbor: Ardis, 1976.

Aksenov, Vasily. *The Steel Bird: And Other Stories*, Rae Slonek, tr. Ann Arbor: Ardis, 1979.

Goscilo, Helena and Byron Lindsey. *Glasnost: An Anthology of Russian Literature under Gorbachev*. Ann Arbor: Ardis, 1990.

Gushchin, E. "Ten Strekoszy" (Shadow of a Dragonfly). *Our Contemporary*, March 1974, pp. 84–101.

Proffer, Carl R., ed. *Contemporary Russian Prose*. Ann Arbor: Ardis, 1982.

Proffer, Carl R. and Proffer, Ellendea. *The Barsukov Triangle, The Two-Toned Blond and Other Stories*. Ann Arbor: Ardis, 1984.

Pushkin, Alexander. *Ruslan and Ludmila*, Walter Arndt, tr. Ann Arbor: Ardis, 1974.

Rasputin, Valentin. *Farewell to Matyora*, Antonina W. Bouis, tr. New York: Macmillan, 1979.

Solzhenitsyn, Alexander. *One Day in the Life of Ivan Denisovich*, H. T. Willetts, tr. New York: Farrar, Straus, Giroux, 1991.

Tolstaya, Tatyana. *On the Golden Porch*, Antonina W. Bouis, tr. New York: Alfred A. Knopf, 1989.

Vishevsky, Anatoly. *Soviet Literary Culture in the 1970s: the Politics of Irony*. Gainsville: University Press of Florida, 1993.

Vladimov, Georgi. *Faithful Ruslan: The Story of a Guard Dog*, Michael Glenny, tr. New York: Simon and Schuster, 1979.

℘

Russian Artists:
From Realism to Freedom

Maria Carlson
University of Kansas, Lawrence, Kansas

Russia has a rich tradition of art, the roots of which are steeped in the spirituality of its spectacular icons and the whimsy of its folk art. Russians have searched for the roots of their identity in their literature, architecture, philosophy, religion, culture, social thought, and most especially in their art. Paintings, books, temples, and icons are documentation of their spiritual and intellectual journey. They contain the Russian history that will help guide them into a Russian future.

In such a setting, where political realities have traditionally forced art and literature to be the principal carriers of the nation's intellectual baggage, the arts could never be mere pastimes or amusements. In a land where poets and artists are heroes, martyrs, and role models, Russians take their arts very seriously.

Russian Art of the Second Half of the Nineteenth Century

Russian non-religious painting developed only in the eighteenth century. For many centuries Russian art was dominated by the tradition of icon painting borrowed by the Russian Orthodox

Church from Byzantium. Not until the reign of Peter the Great (1672–1725) did Western influences in painting and sculpture significantly replace the Byzantine influence. During the eighteenth and early nineteenth centuries, Russian art turned from the Byzantine Church to the European studio, essentially still imitating Western academic models. By the second half of the nineteenth century, however, Russian art caught up with the West, reached a world class level, and began to command attention in its own right.

Like Ivan Turgenev (1818–83), Fyodor Dostoevsky (1821–81), and Leo Tolstoy (1828–1910), the great high-culture Russian realist writers, Russia's painters of the second part of the nineteenth century were deeply interested in social themes. Russian art, like Russian literature, further strengthened its social conscience. The Critical Realist painters Pavel Fedotov (1815–52), Vasily Perov (1833–82), Vasily Surikov (1848–1916) and Ilya Repin (1844–930) documented the plight of the Russian peasants and the urban poor in dramatic scenes showing the stoic suffering of the *insulted and the injured*. Other works satirized the self-satisfied merchant class or clergy who abused their office. Many documented the heroism of the growing revolutionary movement, and still others portrayed important lessons in dramatic moments of the Russian past that needed to be put to use in the present. Even portrait painting attempted to communicate social responsibility, soul-searching, and ethical quandaries through the faces of Russians. The art of the Critical Realists, beneath its realism and purely representational style, was highly ideological. The purpose of this art, like the purpose of Critical Realist literature, was to activate the Russians' social conscience and show them how to live moral and useful lives. It condemned abuses, and praised those who would better the world.

By 1870 some Critical Realists had formed an organization of their own, calling themselves the "Wanderers." This group of progressive artists had voluntarily withdrawn from the stuffiness of the Russian Academy of Arts. They mounted a series of traveling exhibits in order to take art out of the salon to the common people in towns and villages. The Wanderers considered the

Vasily Perov. 'Troika' 1866. The plight of the peasant and the urban poor is the theme of this painting. Perov explores the theme of child labor, likening the children to a 'troika' of work horses.

moral, ethical and narrative aspects of art as important as its aesthetics, and took "Realism, Nationalism, and Social Consciousness" as their credo. Art was to serve humanitarian and social ideals and bring these ideals to the all the Russian people. Thus the art of social commentary, which merged both high culture and popular tastes, dominated Russian painting and literature until the very end of the century.

The Russian Silver Age (1890–1915)

By 1900, the highly ideological and realistic art of the Critical Realists started to give way to the new and exciting modernist trends that shocked viewers in Russia, France and Germany. By the eve of the Bolshevik Revolution, Russian artists had long ago left imitation, apprenticeship, and even realism far behind, and were creating some of the most exciting art anywhere. Emerging from a relatively parochial and constrained nineteenth-century Russian tradition, the Russian modernists burst into an unsuspecting international art world to become giants of modern painting.

In the two decades that preceded the Revolution of 1917, Russia experienced a flowering of the graphic and decorative arts unprecedented in its history. To some extent this new art was a reaction against the social messages and the civic art of the Critical Realists. Exhausted by paintings of suffering peasants and boundless Russian nature, art connoisseurs of the Silver Age thrilled to the opulent and exotic visual fantasies of Mikhail Vrubel (1856–1910), Leonid Bakst (1866–1924), Nikolai Roerich (1874–1947), Alexander Golovin (1863–1930), and Alexander Benois (1870–1960). These were the years of the "World of Art" and Serge Diaghilev's "Ballet Russes." The themes of this art were anything but social commentary: love and death, the demonic, folklore, mythology, and a romanticized and idealized Russian past.

(Tretakov Gallery, Moscow)

Mikhail Vrubel. 'Swan Princess' 1900. By the turn of the century, realist art gave way to new and exciting modernist trends, centered around Mikhail Vrubel and the World of Art Group. Vrubel's 'Swan Princess' tempts the viewer away from harsh reality into the land of folklore and mystery.

The style of the Russian Symbolist painters differed significantly from the high realism of the Critical Realist painters and the Wanderers. The new Symbolists preferred a dreamier, more impressionistic style, with color applied as fuzzy patches in order to catch mood and light rather than represent an object. They also employed stylization and design for their own sake. Although the Symbolists were heavily influenced by cosmopolitan European artistic trends—Impressionism was a generation old in Europe and much in vogue—they did not ignore their Russian roots. They revived the ancient icon style. But they were *not* realistic painters. Their painting, like the avant-garde poetry of the period, attempted to escape mundane reality and to achieve some higher, spiritual plane.

The Symbolists were interested not only in high art, but in the applied arts. They designed clothing, furniture, and patterns for cloth and wallpaper. Some were architects, many were stage and costume designers, and others worked in ceramics and jewelry. Russian Symbolists endeavored to create a total artistic environment, much like the continental practitioners of Art Nouveau, the British pre-Raphaelite, and the "arts and crafts" movement.

Just as Russian Critical Realism in art had been firmly embedded in literary realism, this turn-of-the-century aestheticism also found parallels in the literature, music, and religious philosophy of the period. The exotic, decorative, and mystical themes of Symbolist painting were echoed in the works of the Russian Symbolist writers Valery Briusov (1873–1924), Alexander Blok (1880–1921), and Andrei Bely (1880–1934), the composer Alexander Scriabin (1871/72–1915), and the religious and mystical philosopher Vladimir Solov'iev (1853–1900).

By the eve of the First World War, the decorative and dreamy visions of Symbolism began to give way to the more energetic and strident strokes of the modernist avant-garde. They were influenced by and created hand-in-hand with European post-Impressionism, Primitivism, Cubo-futurism, and abstract painting as practiced by the French modernists Paul Cezanne (1839–1906) and Henri Matisse (1869–1954). The Russian art world quickly splintered into a variety of radical unions, groups, and salons with inventive names: Blue Rose, Donkey's Tail, 0.10, Jack of Diamonds. It was the age of -isms: along with Post-Impressionism, Primitivism, and Cubo-Futurism, there was Futurism, Abstractionism, Suprematism, Constructivism, and Rayonism. Radical experimentation was the concept of the moment as painters explored color, form, movement, and even the fourth dimension in their art.

Like the Symbolist painters, the Russian avant-garde artists were closely allied with literature and the other arts. Futurism, for example, was both an artistic and a poetic movement. Also like the Symbolists, the avant-garde artists were interested in the applied arts, including architecture, illustration, clothing design, posters, theatrical design, and ceramics. Although they were cosmopolitan movements, both Russian Symbolism and the avant-garde retained a sense of unique national identity, despite a strong European influence.

Unlike the historically rooted and mostly apolitical Symbolists, however, many of the avant-garde artists were interested in futurology, science, technology, and the new genres produced by technology, such as photography and cinema. They wanted to destroy the old art in order to create new art, to destroy the old world in order to build a new one. The avant-garde was also politically engaged with the emerging forces of the left, and many intellectually welcomed the Bolshevik Revolution that was to sweep away the decaying tsarist and bourgeois past.

The Revolution and the Avant Garde

Immediately after 1917, Revolutionary Russia was a great place for visionary, revolutionary, and avant-garde artists like Vladimir Tatlin (1885–1953), Kazimir Malevich (1878–1935), and Alexander Rodchenko (1891–1956). As was the case with writers, however, some perceived that they could not create under the new Soviet system. Vasily Kandinsky (1866–1944) and Marc Chagall (1887–1985) were two Russian artists who emigrated and subsequently made their reputations abroad. Like those who stayed, they too had their roots in a heady and dynamic revolutionary atmosphere of artistic fermentation and experimentation. Modernist and

(Russian Museum, St. Petersburg)

Marc Chagall. 'Red Jew' 1915. Marc Chagall made his subsequent career in France, but first brought a new dimension, in form and content, to Russian painting. In 'The Red Jew,' Chagall makes an ambivalent comment about both the initial Jewish support for the Revolution and Jewish identity in Russia.

abstract painters were initially welcomed by the Bolsheviks, put in charge of art institutes, and tasked with creating a New Art for the *New Soviet Man* who would forge and live in the Socialist Utopia.

The post-revolutionary avant-garde held on for less than a decade. By the end of the New Economic Policy in 1928, the increasingly conservative and stodgy Soviet government saw an implicit threat in the avant-garde. Their creative individualism, elitism, and experimentation, their passion for the non-objective and the abstract, and their commitment to an on-going radical transformation of the social fabric of Russia, made them an enemy of the totalitarian status quo, a distraction for a nation about to re-industrialize.

The avant-garde is by nature daring, disruptive, and revolutionary. It constantly teeters on the very cutting edge of culture, and frequently evokes excessive behavior on the part of its adherents, such as wearing odd clothes, painting faces yellow, or walking lobsters on a leash—all of which the Russian avant-garde did. The avant-garde loathes tradition and stability. It is

(Tretakov Gallery, Moscow)

Vasily Kandinsky. 'Improvisation on Cold Forms' 1914. Kandinsky's representational work soon gave way to 'pure' painting, liberated from the dictates of realistic representation. This dynamic improvisation uses color and abstract shapes to convey Kandinsky's subjective sense of his subject.

contemptuous both of society as a whole and of the artistic marketplace. It takes pleasure in shaking up and taunting what it perceives as the status quo. The anarchic and individualist Russian avant-garde could not exist for long in the puritanical and collectivist environment of Stalin's new Soviet Union. It did not disappear altogether, however, but went abroad or into "internal exile."

An artistic counter-movement to the extremism and abstractionism of the avant-garde appeared by the early 1920s. These representational artists, some of them former students of avant-garde painters, chose to paint the present-day, real-life concerns of Russian peasants, workers, revolutionaries, and soldiers. They combined creative composition and bold use of color and light with traditional techniques to document the achievements and hopes of the fledgling Soviet Union. Artists like Kuzma Petrov-Vodkin (1878–1939), Isaak Brodsky (1884–1939), Alexander Deineka (1899–1969), and Yuri Pimenov (1903–1977) produced objective paintings which were more accessible and considerably more appealing to the masses than the elitist and mostly incomprehensible experiments of the avant-garde. Not surprisingly, these "revolutionary realists" were the heralds of what would really become the politically correct *New Art* as defined by Stalin.

Between 1928 and 1932, Russia experienced a second cultural revolution. By 1932, an attempt was made to bring all creative activities, including art and literature, under the control of the state. The individual republics of the Soviet Union began to create national artists unions, such as the Union of Russian Artists and the Union of Ukrainian Artists. These were eventually brought together into the gargantuan Union of Artists of the USSR. This Union, a counter-part to the notorious Writers Union, was the compliant servant of the Party and officially-sanctioned vehicle of the *New Art*. As such, it became the final arbiter of artistic taste.

The unionization of the arts in the Soviet Union terminated the natural development of Russian modern art and redefined

(Tretakov Gallery, Moscow)

Kuzma Petrov-Vodkin. "The Year 1918 in Petrograd'"1920. In this work which came to be called "The Petrograd Madonna," Petrov-Vodkin uses the traditional icon composition of the "tender Madonna." Even the mother's white scarf, wrapped around her head, evokes the enlarged head of the Madonna in traditonal Byzantine icons, while her features resemble those elongated and refined facial features of that genre. The baby is a child born of revolution.

(Central Lenin Museum, Moscow)

Isaak Brodsky. "Lenin in the Smolny Institute" 1930. Known to evry Soviet citizen, Brodsky's introspective, private painting of Lenin contributed to his mythology.

the artist's role in Soviet society. No longer a connoisseur or creative spirit, the artist was now a *shock worker in art* and, like his literary peers, an *engineer of human souls*. The face of Russian art was forcibly turned back to the highly ideological Critical Realism that dominated the second half of the nineteenth century. But there was a difference. Late nineteenth-century Critical Realists had been motivated by their own social conscience. Now a mandated and artificially imposed official state ideology dictated who would paint and what would be seen.

This official turn to the past separated Russian art from artistic developments in the West, and completely isolated it from the give and take of the international art world. Russian art fell victim to inbreeding and provincialism. The Soviet state denounced Western developments as decadent, bourgeois, and subversive, and prevented its artists from having any intercourse with them. A prudish intolerance was felt everywhere in the Soviet culture, but particularly in art.

Why did Russian artists tolerate this situation? Simply, they had no choice. If one was to be formally recognized as an artist, to have access to canvas and paint in a country where art supplies were in short supply, or to obtain space to exhibit work and a gallery to broker it, one had to be a member of the Union. The cost of membership was clearly stated: in order to belong to the Union, you had to follow its guidelines and you had to assume the proper ideological position in the style and content of your art. By 1932 Russian art, literature, and all other creative activities were under the thumb of the state, and Socialist Realism became the official artistic ideology.

Socialist Realism

Socialist Realism was defined as a creative method expressing the socialist vision of the world and mankind. Its purpose was to contribute to the creation of a socialist society and to *educate the workers in the spirit of communism.* Both form and content had to reflect socialist ideals and *depict reality in its revolutionary development.* Socialist Realist paintings of contemporary events showed

(Tretakov Gallery, Moscow)

Serafima Riangina. "Ever Higher" 1934. The paintings of Serafima Riangina are quintessential socialist realism. Her powerfully-built heroes and heroines are always striving for as yet unconquered heights, as in this socialist realist classic.

the clash between the old bourgeois and the new socialist worlds. They depicted man as a fighter for and creator of a new society. The term "Socialist Realism" evokes images of the paintings of Stalin's favorite painter Sergei Gerasimov (1885–1964), as well as Arkadii Plastov (1893–1972), and Serafima Riangina (1891–1955), known as the Soviet Norman Rockwell. Socialist Realism images contained robust young women with strong legs, proudly gathering abundant golden sheaves of grain, waving at airplanes in the vivid blue Soviet skies. Or they were of Lenin, looking fearlessly into the Radiant Future as he lectured heroically from a banner-draped platform to clear-eyed, serious, obviously inspired workmen and soldiers. They portrayed muscular workers in a state of exhilaration, climbing ever higher up a high voltage tower. From 1932 until the mid-1980s, Socialist Realism meant health, enthusiasm, heroism, optimism, bright colors, and shamelessly flattering portraits of mythologized leaders.

The Counter-Culture: The Ideology of Anti-Ideology

As was the case with writers, the regimentation of creativity and the "unionization" of artists led inevitably to the emergence of an anti-culture. This anti-culture emerged as a counter balance just as political regimentation created an active political dissident movement, and the rigid centralized economy produced a flourishing black market. This is the essence of the "cultural schizophrenia" most Westerners sense when studying Soviet Russian society. The stranglehold of the Artists Union on such an individualistic product as a painting produced a deep division within Russian art, leading to the creation of "official" and "unofficial" artists and art movements.

The seeds of unofficial art as an initial movement sprouted after the death of Stalin in 1953. Everything was changed by that event—even the face of Socialist Realism. Artists and writers, ever sensitive to changes in official policy, soon sensed a "thaw" in the icy relations between State and Art. After years of the worst excesses of Socialist Realism, writers and painters were encouraged to look again at the work of the past and rediscover their own history. Works once banned were now cautiously allowed.

Parts of the Russian modernist heritage were acknowledged in a series of exhibits by previously banned artists. These exhibits, however, were not open to the general public, but only to official art specialists, approved by the regime, and to interested Party elite. The average Russian knew nothing of them at all.

One of the events that, ironically, gave the unofficial art movement some cohesiveness was *Thirty Years of Moscow Art*, an exhibition that opened at the Manezh in Moscow in the late fall of 1962. It was attended by Nikita Khrushchev, who was appalled at the general digression from the Socialist Realist order. Every word out of Khrushchev's mouth revealed his total lack of aesthetic understanding, his ignorance of the artistic tradition, and his lack of sympathy with the creative act. But in the Soviet Union, the General Secretary "was always right." Although the exhibit had considerable public support and attracted an unprecedented number of generally satisfied viewers, an obligatory public breast-beating followed at the Artists Union for permitting such a thing to happen. Nevertheless, the genie was out of the Stalinist bottle

After Khrushchev's removal in 1964, there were a few years of uneasy calm before a new and different kind of repression emerged under Brezhnev. Members of the Artists Union re-evaluated their own role in Soviet art. Some began to live double lives. They would cynically create one kind of art on demand to provide a meal ticket, and another kind of art for their own pleasure and aesthetic need. Cynicism was to become the hallmark of the Brezhnev years, called the *Period of Stagnation.*

The counter-culture art movement had, at best, poor access to its own artistic heritage. For many years, Russian modernist paintings had been either sold abroad, destroyed, or put away into storage and never exhibited. The Russian artistic underground dealt with this deprivation in various ways, notably through private collections, really "private museums." Some incredible collections were taken out of the Soviet Union and exhibited in other countries, and fine "apartment collections" were held by others. In this way, the heritage of Russian art was preserved during the years of Soviet rule.

It is important to note that during these same years, Russian artists in general, but unofficial artists in particular, were cut off from direct dialogue with the international art community. Unable to enjoy the travel and fraternization privileges that Union members had, unofficial artists had no direct contact with Western developments. They were not ignorant of Western art, but they knew it selectively, and sometimes accidentally, from illustrations in art books, from smuggled slides, and from rare visiting art exhibits from abroad. Their only direct sources of materials came from the Russian émigré communities in Paris, New York, Los Angeles, and Rome. These artists abroad had unlimited access to everything and sent materials back to their colleagues in the Soviet Union. This helped to broaden the unofficial artists understanding of Western art through conscious selection, and not simply through chance encounter.

Boris Menkovsky. "The City" (early 1980s). Counter-culture painting often "cites" Russian literary or historical reality, but it bears no resemblance to official Russian classics. A face, a nose, a spire, thick fog—this work evokes the surreal and threatening city (Petersburg) of the writer Nikolai Gogel.

The unofficial artists' relative isolation from the international community, and even from the official art within their own country, is reflected in their work. Tremendous variety, freshness and creativity are apparent in the best of contemporary Russian unofficial artists, such as Ilya Kabakov (1933–), Erik Bulatov (1933–), Tatiana Nazarenko (1944–), and Olga Bulgakova (1951–). In spite of the limitations, hardships, and repression they experienced, unofficial Soviet artists produced a remarkable variety of different styles, each more esoteric than the other. They indulged in Photo-Realism, Primitivism, Surrealism, *Sotsart* (ironic and cynical parodies of Socialist Realism), Conceptualism, the New Metaphysics, Abstract Expressionism, different levels and forms of abstraction, iconography, folk art and "Citation Art."

The only consistency in their art was "individual self-expression," the central concept toward which all new artists moved. But the form and subject matter of their self-expression varied. A visitor to an exhibit of the "Moscow 20" might have concluded that in one picture, the artist thought he was Vrubel', and in another he pretended to be Matisse. At first glance, such paintings appeared superficially imitative. But they were not imitative They were an aesthetic "citation" to and endorsement of Vrubel' or Matisse that established both the artist's sense of continuity in art and his right to belong to and participate in the entire artistic tradition from which he had been artificially and politically excluded.

This dialogue between the past and the present is an immensely important dimension of contemporary Russian art, as well as contemporary literature and cinema. One needs only see *glasnost'* films like *Repentance* or read literary works like Trifonov's posthumously published *Disappearance* or Dombrovsky's *Department of Unnecessary Things* to recognize the importance of such a dialogue. This explains the passion for publishing Pasternak's *Doctor Zhivago*, Evgeny Zamiatin's *We*, and Alexander Solzhenitsyn's novels. All are the legitimate birthright of the Russian people that has been kept from them by the powers that were.

But what will happen to the future of underground opposition art when the underground itself is gone? *Glasnost'* has come to art at last. There is even a new word for it, *artnost'*, which refers to the freedom to paint as *glasnost'* refers to the freedom to speak out. What will happen now that the political, ethical, and cultural conditions that produced underground art appear to be disappearing, or at least changing?

For one thing, a certain nostalgia for the times of repression has already appeared. "Life is no longer interesting.""Nobody visits my studio anymore." Gone are the wonderful days of confusion and new terminology, the days of "passwords" known only to a few, when someone becomes your intimate because he, too, has heard of post-modernism and has read the latest issue of *A-IA* (A to Z, a French journal devoted to the contemporary Russian avant-garde). Today, you can pick up *Ogonek*, the Soviet answer to *Life Magazine*, distributed by the millions, and see an entire article on Ernst Neizvestny (1955–) or Vitaly Komar (1943–) and Alexander Melamid (1945–). The mere names of such counter-culture artists were considered an abomination in the Soviet Union after their emigration in the late 1970s.

Today's relative openness and freedom in the Russian art world is certain to have a tremendous impact on the counter-culture artists and their art. Their creative impulse was born of opposition and fueled by alienation, anger, resentment, and the excitement of playing life-and-death games. What will inspire them when their only dictator is poverty?

It is both provocative and ironic that nothing new or major has emerged from either *glasnost'* or *artnost'*. Much contemporary art could even be termed "repression epigonism"—an art form which expresses nostalgia for itself and repeats already developed themes. As *glasnost'* has not yet produced the great post-Soviet novel or play, *artnost'* has not yet produced the great post-Soviet painting or a major new art trend. Like every other thing in Russian society, art is too busy trying to understand where it is to deal with an unfamiliar flood of information. It must first learn to cope with the ominous tremors shaking society as a whole.

At the same time, counter-culture artists have had to cope with exploitation by Western galleries. They have to deal, for the first time, with the seduction of "big bucks" and the tension that comes when they face that blank canvas and decide whether they are going to be true to themselves (maybe the buyer won't like it) or commercial (imitate an artist whose work sells well). They do not even have the advantage of an organized domestic art market to help compile, evaluate and market their work.

One of the things that made Russian underground art so interesting was that it was created as pure self-expression, as a statement that precisely located the artist in his society. Much of it was created without any hope of sale, without any possibility of exhibition. Rather, it came from a sense of moral and aesthetic right. It was also created without the fear of rejection in a free art marketplace.

And what will happen when the novelty, the exotic patina of Russian art wears off? When the jaded Western market, fickle and faddish, finds a new *cause celebre*, or else decides that Russian art is too difficult, too culture-specific in an international market, and thus only of limited interest? As if to demonstrate this historical irony, collectors today are avidly acquiring old Socialist Realist paintings—the more Stalinist the better—just as they once tried to ferret out the best counter-culture art.

Full Circle: The Ironic Legacy of Contemporary Russian Art

The Period of Stagnation (1966-82) ironically turned out to be the beginning of a Period of Reclamation, a time when certain parts of the Russian cultural past were quietly led out of their unofficial exile. Today this period of Reclamation is in full swing. What we are observing is the reacquaintance of Russian culture as a whole with its own artificially deformed art tradition, and with the entire march of Western European and world art. As events have permitted the reclamation of Russia's pre-revolutionary cultural past, they have also opened the floodgates of memory and history. This all leads back to one important point when Russia's creativity, culture and thought were ruthlessly and prematurely cut off by the demands of political expediency. Returning to the time before the void is essential. Only in this way can Russians pick up and complete the natural lines of development that were not allowed to reach maturity.

Russian culture is returning to thoughts, trends and ideas of the 1920s, for example, which were unfinished, artificially prevented from achieving fruition. The wonderful discovery for us might be that the natural line of Russian artistic development that flowered so luxuriously at the turn of the century has not died. Hopefully, it has only been in suspension, the breath of its creativity held in by private collectors, unofficial artists, historical curators, and the emigration, waiting to be released.

Nicholas Berdiaev, a philosopher from the beginning of the century, predicted that *the consequences of the creative spiritual surge of the beginning of the twentieth century cannot be annihilated, much of it remains, and will, some time in the future, be restored.* We may be seeing the beginnings of that restoration today in literature, in philosophical thought, and in the arts.

Suggested Readings

Bowlt, John. *Russian Art of the Avant Garde*. Revised and enlarged. New York: Thames and Hudson, 1988.

Brown, Matthew Cullern. *Contemporary Russian Art*. New York: Philosophical Library/Phaidon Press, 1989.

Elliot, David. *New Worlds. Russian Art and Society 1900–1937*. New York: Rizzoli, 1976.

Gray, Camilla. *The Russian Experiment in Art 1863–1922*. London: Thames and Hudson, 1968.

Rice, Tamara Talbot. *A Concise History of Russian Art*. London: Thames and Hudson, 1963.

A-IA: Contomporary Russian Art. Journal, manifestos and articles.

Paintings from the Russian Museum Collection. Leningrad: Aurora, 1975.

Russian Avant-Garde and Soviet Contemporary Art. Geneva: Sotheby's, 1988.

Russian and Soviet Paintings 1900 to 1930 [Catalog of the Hirshhorn Museum, Smithsonian Institution, July 17 to September 25, 1988]. Washington: Smithsonian Institution Press, 1988.

The George Costakis Collection: Russian Avant-Garde. New York: Abrams, 1981.

The Tretakov Gallery: Painting: Leningrad: Aurora, 1976.

Women in Russia:
Images and Realities

Barbara Evans Clements
University of Akron, Akron, Ohio

The Images

In the 1980s the Wendy's restaurant chain ran a commercial on television that featured a stout, middle-aged woman who thought she was a fashion model. In the first scene she strutted back and forth across the stage in an ugly flowered dress, while the voice of a male announcer with a heavy Russian accent intoned, "Day Wear." In the next scene, she was still striding up and down the runway, but now she was carrying an industrial-size flashlight. The announcer said sternly, "Evening Wear." In the next and final scene, she was carrying a beach ball. "Beach Wear," the announcer declared. In all three scenes, the woman, who looked so proud of herself, was wearing the same plain dress.

It hard to remember now, almost a decade later, what all this had to do with hamburgers, but it is easy to remember what the commercial said about Soviet women. They were too stupid to realize how dowdy they were. The Wendy's ad, coming just as Mikhail Gorbachev and Ronald Reagan were making the breakthroughs in diplomacy that ended the Cold War, summed up a lot of American ideas about the Soviet Union. Many of us thought that the USSR, like the Wendy's woman, was big, dumb, and ugly, and unjustifiably proud of itself.

Americans had other ideas about the Russians, and they too showed up in our images of their women. In the espionage novels of Ian Fleming, John Le Carre, and Tom Clancy (to name only the most famous), there were a lot of Soviet female spies. These women could not have been more unlike the Wendy's woman. They were beautiful, intelligent, highly educated, and deadly, unless they could be persuaded to fall in love with their enemy—the competent, powerful American or Englishman.

Both the Wendy's woman and the sexy spy were fictional creations. But there were some real Soviet women that worked their way into our minds before 1991. A couple were Soviet first ladies. In the 1950s there was Nina Khrushcheva, wife of First Secretary of the Communist Party Nikita Khrushchev. She was kind and matronly, but she did look a lot like the Wendy's woman. Quite different was Raisa Gorbacheva, Gorbachev's wife. She showed us how far the Soviet Union had come since the 1950s. She was stylish, well educated, and poised when the bright lights of the international press were turned on her.

But the real Soviet women we saw most often were the athletes. In the 1950s and 1960s the press paid a lot of attention to brawny female shot-putters and track-and-field competitors. Later, in the 1970s and 1980s, these bulky and anonymous women (we rarely knew them by name) gave way in sports coverage to more feminine Soviet women, the figure skaters and gymnasts. They were highly competitive, like the spies in the novels, but watching them close up helped us get to know them. We learned their names and we saw that many of them were sweet, innocent girls who cried when they lost. Perhaps our sympathetic view of these women was a sign, not much noted at the time, that the Cold War was ending.

What was the reality behind these somewhat contradictory images of Soviet women? How typical were the Wendy's woman, the clever spy, the beautiful skater, of real women in the USSR or in today's Russia? To explore the realities behind the images we must first look back at the history of women in the Soviet Union, then next consider the women of contemporary Russia. What we will find is that while our images had some truth in them, they are much simpler, and really much less interesting, than reality.

The Realities: Women's History in the USSR

Before the 1917 Revolution:
Poor, Burdened and Unequal

The Wendy's woman and the figure skater had this in common: they worked hard. That is true of Russian women today, and it has been true for many centuries. Not every woman in Russia was Russian, for there was a great diversity of ethnic groups in that huge empire before the revolution of 1917. The largest of these "nationalities," as they were called, were the Russians, Ukrainians, Belorussians, Lithuanians, Estonians, Latvians, Finns, Tatars, and Jews of the western part of the country, the Georgians, Armenians, and Azerbaidzhanis of the Caucasus region, and the Kazakhs, Uzbeks, Kirgiz, Turkmen, and Tadziks of Central Asia. There were also other, smaller nationalities scattered across this vast country. These peoples differed enormously from one another in religion, customs, and history, but the majority of them, upwards of 85 percent as late as 1917, were poor farmers, that is, peasants. They were poor because Russia has always been a difficult place in which to get rich. The government and the nobility exploited ordinary people. The environment, too, was hard on people.

The peasants had to work hard in order to survive, so they did not have the luxury of believing that women should stay home and take care of the house. Peasant women worked in the fields planting and harvesting crops, they gathered mushrooms and berries, they carried water, they tended livestock, they made clothes, they did most of the family's cooking, and of course they bore and raised children. Men prized women for their work, but all the many ethnic groups also believed that God had intended women to take orders from men. Thus women in Russia before the revolution suffered from a dual burden: most of them were poor and all of them, the rich ones and the poor, were thought to be less intelligent and even less moral than men.

In the 1920s and 1930s: Educated and Overworked

The communist government established in 1917 made a sincere effort to better women's lives. The communists thought they were going to improve Russia for everyone by abolishing all the old beliefs, among them the notion that women were inferior. To achieve this they used the mass media to promote the idea that women should be men's equals. They also opened the schools to girls and set up job-training programs for women, for they believed that women could be freed from inequality only if they did the same work as men. To relieve women from the burdens of housework and childcare, the communist government established daycare centers, restaurants, and laundries.

Women took advantage of these new opportunities enthusiastically. In the 1920s and especially in the 1930s they streamed into the schools and into the workplaces of the rapidly growing economy. In 1926, 74 percent of city women and only 35 percent of rural women in the Soviet Union could read and write. By 1939 these figures had risen to 91 percent of city women and 77 percent of rural women. Women made up over 80 percent of those people joining the paid work force for the first time in the 1930s. By the end of that decade, they were 57 percent of farm workers and 38 percent of white- and blue-collar workers.[1]

The Soviet government kept its promise to educate women, then get them jobs in factories and offices, but it did not do nearly as much to help them with housework. Public laundries, inexpensive restaurants, and daycare centers did spring up in the major cities, but there were not enough of them in the 1930s to meet people's needs. The government believed that it had to spend most of its money on heavy industry, so it shortchanged the entire consumer sector of the economy, not just daycare centers, but also housing, transportation, waste disposal, all the necessities of urban life. Meanwhile people were flooding into the cities to find jobs, swelling the demand for these necessities even while the supply stayed low. As a result life was hard in urban as well as rural areas, and women continued to do most of the housekeeping and childcare in addition to their paying jobs.

Conditions were also difficult in the 1930s because the Soviet Union was a dictatorship. Although the constitution declared that the government was elected by the people and that everyone had civil rights, in reality Communist Party officials made all the important decisions. And they were cruel. In the late 1920s and early 1930s they forced peasants to surrender their land to government control. Millions of people died in the resulting violence and famine. Later in the 1930s, Stalin, as head of the Communist Party, ordered purges that resulted in more millions of deaths and imprisonments. Women did not lead any of these catastrophes, because the Communist Party and the political police were headed by men, but women suffered the awful consequences: some starved, many lost loved ones, some were arrested themselves. Consequently, the 1930s was a time of great economic achievements in the Soviet Union, but also of great insecurity and hardship.

During World War II: Sacrificing and Significant

Life only got harder during World War II. Adolf Hitler's armies attacked the USSR on June 22, 1941, setting off a struggle that eventually took the lives of 27 million Soviet citizens. It was a monstrous war in which women played a very important part. More than one million served in the military, mostly as support personnel—doctors, nurses, truck drivers, and communication experts. Some women fought at the front: they flew fighters, drove tanks, and sniped at German patrols. Meanwhile millions of women kept industry going to supply the troops. By the end of war women made up 57 percent of the nonagricultural labor force and 80 percent of all collective farmers. They worked long hours with no holidays for weeks on end, getting by mostly on bread and whatever vegetables they could grow and preserve themselves. By 1945 millions of women had died from combat and disease, but the sacrifices of all of them meant the difference between defeat and victory. When the war was finally over, they stayed at work, now rebuilding the shattered country.[2]

Between 1953 and 1985: Proud, Professional and Discontent

Life began to improve for ordinary Soviet women in the 1950s. After Stalin's death in 1953 a new group of communist leaders came to power, men determined not to repeat the worst excesses of the dead dictator's reign. Perhaps the most important of their reforms for women were the efforts they made to build up the consumer sector of the economy. Although the governments of Nikita Khrushchev (1955–64) and Leonid Brezhnev (1964–82) still spent a lot of money on heavy industry and military hardware, they also increased the supply of daycare centers, food stores, apartments, appliances, and clothes. Women became better educated and more of them moved into white-collar jobs as clerks, salespeople, and teachers. Women were also present in substantial numbers in the professions, particularly in medicine, but also in engineering, architecture, and the academic world.

There were limitations to all this positive change. Women did not make great gains in political power, and the Communist Party remained a dictatorship headed by men. Life was still difficult for all but the most privileged. Even in the cities women continued to do most of the housework with little help from their husbands and with few labor-saving appliances such as washing machines or refrigerators. Women worked even harder in the countryside, for their houses had few amenities and they spent long hours in the fields. By the 1960s women in the USSR enjoyed a standard of living roughly comparable to that in the United States fifty years before. But as long as they measured their lives against all the hardship they had overcome, they had much cause for pride.

In the 1970s, however, standards began to change. A new generation came of age, with higher expectations for their lives, at the very time that economic improvement slowed. The inefficiencies of the excessively centralized Soviet system were beginning to act as a brake on further development. The Party leaders enjoyed fairly comfortable lives, but of course knowing that only fed the discontents of ordinary people. So the Brezhnev leadership decided to let consumer goods come into the country to satisfy growing demand. It sought increased trade with Western Europe and North America and it permitted a black market to develop in clothing, electronics, cosmetics and other luxuries. All these products educated Soviet people to the differences between their standard of living and that of the more prosperous industrialized nations. This new knowledge made them more discontented. By 1980 Soviet women, particularly those who lived in the big cities, were complaining often about the miserable quality of the products in the shops. They were also angry about all the work they still had to do. Vera Golubeva, a woman from the far northern city of Arkhangelsk, wrote this dismal description of the burdens of women's daily lives in 1979.

> Tired after their workday, they hurry home to child care centers. Bowed with the weight of grocery bags, they drag their children behind them. In a terrible crush of people, they wedge themselves into overcrowded public buses, elbowing people aside and pushing their way through to an empty seat, if there is one. At last they reach home. Here, new cares await them: dinner must be prepared and the husband and children must be fed. The laundry and housecleaning still await because, for a working woman, there is no other time for these chores. She cannot depend on her husband for anything.[3]

During the Gorbachev Years, 1985–91: Activists and Feminists

By 1985 unhappiness over the inadequacies of the Soviet economy had reached the very top ranks of the Communist Party itself. The Party had promised the Soviet people the good life, and in the mid-'80s, it was not delivering. So the new generation of communists that came to power with Mikhail Gorbachev in 1985 experimented with economic reform. When more conservative communists blocked these efforts, Gorbachev called for democratizing the political system. Freedom of the press and assembly were permitted, then new legislatures were established. In foreign policy Gorbachev and his foreign minister Edvard Shevardnadze ended the Cold War by signing nuclear disarmament treaties with the United States and by permitting the unpopular communist governments of Eastern Europe to fall.

Unfortunately all the amazing reforms launched by the Gorbachev regime did very little to improve the lives of Soviet women. The new rulers found it far easier to open up the press than to make over their unyielding economy, so they were unable to relieve the burdens women bore. Women still stood in lines for hours every day to buy basic commodities, carried heavy bags home up long flights of steps to crowded apartments, washed clothes in the sink and dried them on lines strung up in the kitchen, all after an eight-hour day on the job. Gorbachev and the other leaders of his government made speeches about the difficulties women endured and set up task forces to study them, but such talk would not produce needed goods and services.

Nor did the new leadership think very carefully about women's situation. They did not question the old Stalinist ideas that women should be workers outside and inside the home. Nor did they discuss ways to give women more equality with men. The men leading the reform process understood that the inadequacies of the society had placed an unduly heavy load on women, but they thought, as had communist leaders from the very beginning of the USSR, that they would solve women's problems by reforming the entire society. At some time in the future everything would be made right. For now, the male leaders would decide what needed to be done. A growing number of Soviet women were fed up with this approach. Irina Valkeva, a cashier in Moscow, poured out the widespread exasperation to a British interviewer in 1990:

> You know, all of those people who were talking of such matters, almost every one of them was a man. Men discussing how to improve the lot of Soviet women, and scarcely a woman's voice or opinion to be heard. . . . There's very little awareness in Russia that women's views need even to be heard.[4]

But women did speak out in the passionate debates over how to reform the Soviet Union that went on in the 1980s. They published critical articles in the press, organized self-help groups in the cities, raised money for the poor, restored churches, and participated in political parties. Women were prominent leaders of the independence movements in the Baltic states and Ukraine. And high on their agendas was what to do to make the society work better for women.

Many of these activists were very critical of the Communist Party's policies. Sociologist Tatiana Zaslavskaia and novelist

Tatiana Tolstaia, among many others, charged that the communist government had never really cared about making women free, but had only wanted to put them to work for the system. "Women have been manipulated throughout most of our history," declared philologist Larisa Kuznetsova, "put on tractors, or on steam engines or dropped out of planes with parachutes." Instead she argued that emancipation must be created by women themselves. But what were women to do? These critics gave different answers. Some were feminists who wanted women fully involved in the society as men's equals; others thought they would make life better by devoting their energies to their families. All agreed, though, that the situation was getting worse, not better. And all agreed with Irina Valkeva that the male leadership was talking, but not listening.

Developments Since 1991: Discrimination and Disillusionment

The Soviet Union came to an end in December 1991, with the establishment of the Confederation of Independent States. Change has continued since then in Russia, with very mixed results. In general the news for women—farm workers and city-dwellers, Siberians and Muscovites—has not been good. They have lost, or are in danger of losing, many of the benefits of the old Soviet system without gaining much from the new society. Their basic problem— too many burdens and too few opportunities—has not changed at all. In fact, for many individual women, it has only gotten worse.

Women throughout Russia are suffering because the economy has continued to deteriorate. A few people have benefited from the new entrepreneurial opportunities, but the great majority of the population has only seen life become more difficult. Rampant inflation has wiped out savings. Government financing of such amenities as vacation hotels on the Black Sea has dried up. There are fewer lines at the shops now, but this is mainly because most people cannot afford to buy the fancy imported goods for sale there. Life is particularly hard for the millions of single older women trying to survive on tiny pensions. Meanwhile, national funding for social services such as daycare and medical clinics has been cut, throwing responsibility for these programs onto local governments already struggling to make ends meet.

The economic collapse is also worsening discrimination against women. Despite their history of participating in the labor force, despite their high levels of education and training, women have been much more likely to lose their jobs than men. Russian statisticians estimate that more than 70 percent of those workers laid off in the current restructuring of government departments and factories are women. Women are less likely than men to be admitted to retraining programs. Some observers also have charged that many women still working have taken pay cuts and are now paid significantly less than men for the same work. Nor are great opportunities available in the new enterprises opening up in Russia. Only 10 percent of the new business owners are women. Foreign companies openly discriminate against women, particularly older ones, in hiring. Moscow newspapers now carry advertisements that specify that those applying for jobs should be between 18 and 25, should look good in a miniskirt, and should be willing to accommodate their bosses' sexual interests.[6]

Politically men still dominate. Boris Yeltsin's cabinet and the leaders of the opposition parties that so bitterly oppose him are all men. In the earliest of the new legislatures established in Russia, the Baltics, Ukraine, the Caucasus and Central Asia, female representation was minuscule, no more than 5 percent. As troubling was a widespread sense among Russia's citizens that women did not belong in politics. People told pollsters that women had disgraced themselves by voting for the Party line in the old, rubber-stamp Soviet parliaments. The fact that all the male delegates to those organizations had voted as they were told did not seem to disqualify men from office-holding.

The prejudice against women in power grew out of deeply held beliefs about women in Russian culture. Before the revolution, Russians had believed that women should tend to their families and leave running the society to men. Men were rational and suited to the hurly-burly of politics, women were gentle and fulfilled when at home. Communists had disputed these ideas, arguing instead that women should be involved in every aspect of society. The Soviet government never provided the support women needed to make this vision a reality, and it never promoted women to the top of the Party. But it had never renounced the idea that women should be equal either. Once communism collapsed, the old ideas about the fundamental differences between women and men seemed to reassert themselves, strengthened now by the widespread disillusionment with communism's failures. Rejection of communism led many women to reject notions of women's equality they associated with it, and turn inward, concentrating on their families. As the economy worsened and the politicians fought with one another, this made a good deal of sense anyway.

Some women have challenged the new discrimination, however, and they may hold the key to the future. Recently more have become active in national politics. The State Duma, the lower house of the parliament elected in December 1993, has 60 female members, or 13.6 percent of the total of 440. It also contains a new political organization entitled Women of Russia, which is pledged to make women's issues its main priority. Women of Russia received 8 percent of the vote cast in December 1993, not an inconsiderable figure considering the fact that they began campaigning very late.[7]

Tens of thousands of women have been setting up self-help groups, a very promising development in a nation where the leaders have long discouraged independent organizations. Hundreds of such organizations existed by early 1994. There are religious societies, support groups for the unemployed, clubs for soldiers' wives, professional organizations for women in business or academics, neighborhood or city-wide associations promoting economic development or providing social services. In Moscow in the late 1980s female sociologists opened The Center for Gender Studies to promote scholarship on women's situation. Recently female professionals have organized The Women's Liberal Movement to fund women-run projects all over the country. Outside Moscow, The Association of Small Towns promotes economic development by marketing local crafts, many of which are made by women.

(All photos courtesy of *Independent Newspaper from Russia, Inc.*)

In their diversity of culture, perspective and ability to cope, the women of Russia are far more interesting than any simple image that might be created from myth or illusion.

(All photos courtesy of Independent Newspaper from Russia, Inc.)

The biggest of all these women-centered organizations is the Union of Women of Russia, the group that sponsored the new political party, Women of Russia. This Union, started in the Soviet days, was originally the Soviet Women's Committee and was composed of prominent women who did propaganda for the government. Given new independence and many new members under Gorbachev, the Committee began to call for attention to women's needs. In 1990 it renamed itself the Union of Women of Russia. Since then it has concentrated on finding work for the unemployed as well as on establishing itself as a national umbrella organization that will put all the women's groups in touch with one another. Some female activists charge that the Union's leaders want to run everything from Moscow. Many women are also very suspicious of politics in general. But of all the hundreds of organizations now active in Russia, only the Union has the connections and the ambition to launch a national effort to get the attention of the squabbling politicians in Moscow.

Living in the Void

The situation of women in Russia today makes one ask, "Has the country really had a revolution?" A new political system has yet to stabilize. Economic reform is ongoing, but slow, and its major effects to date have worsened women's lives. Although communism, the Soviet's official belief system, has fallen into disgrace, no new belief system has emerged to take its place. In the void old ideas about women are pushing back into prominence. Vladimir Zhirinovsky, the ultra-nationalist member of Parliament, recently announced his solution to women's problems: *Our party will find husbands for all unmarried women.*[8]

Consequently the realities of women's lives in today's Russia are not pleasant ones. Political freedom rings hollow when democratically elected leaders cannot solve the nation's problems any better than the communists could. Most women are responding in a time-honored Russian way: they hunker down and take pride in coping with the demands of everyday life. But a few are arguing that women should apply their abilities to the public world, should vote and run for office, should clean up Russia. In the spring of 1993 a columnist in the magazine *Rabotnitsa* called on women to vote for female candidates because women *are used to making peace, to agreeing, and to doing concrete acts of good.* If women get involved, she argued: *Who knows, maybe then our history will finally become a history of happy and rich people.*[9]

Our images of Soviet women were shaped by the fears of the Cold War. Now those fears have receded. The Wendy's woman disappeared years ago and the sexy spies no longer drape themselves across our television screens, except in fading reruns. What will fill the space they took in our impressions of Russia? Which of our new notions about that country will shape our views of the women there? It is too soon to tell. Perhaps we should do away with all images, for they are always too simple to be true. Instead we should get to know real women by reading about their lives and listening to their voices. The women of Russia need our understanding and compassion, not our assumptions and stereotypes. They are, after all, not so different from women all over the world. In their diversity of culture, perspective and ability to cope, they are far more interesting than any simple image that might be created from myth or illusion.

Endnotes

[1]These statistics come from *Women of the U.S.S.R.: Statistical Collection.* Moscow, 1975, pp. 55, 27; and Barbara Evans Clements, *Daughters of Revolution: A History of Women in the USSR.* Arlington Heights, IL: Harlan Davidson, 1994, pp. 71–77.

[2]The statistics in this paragraph come from Clements, *Daughters of Revolution*, pp. 81–87.

[3]Tatyana Mamonova, ed., *Women and Russia: Feminist Writings from the Soviet Union.* Boston: Beacon, 1984, p. 27.

[4]Tony Parker, *Russian Voices.* New York: Henry Holt, 1991, p. 269.

[5]Nina Belyaeva, "Feminism in the USSR," *Canadian Woman Studies.* Winter, 1989, p. 18.

[6]The New York Times, April 17,1994, 1; Nadezhda Os'minina, "Russia is Masculine in Gender," *Woman Worker.* May 1993, p. 10–11; Yevgenia Arbats, "Russia: Women on the Edge," *Ms.* March-April 1994, p. 12.

[7]Nadezhda Shvedova, "Women in Politics: The Federal Assembly Election Results, 1993 Russia," paper read at the Annual Meeting of the International Studies Association, Washington, D.C., 1993, p. 7.

[8]Albats, "Russia: Women on the Edge," p. 15.

[9]Os'minina, "Russia is Masculine in Gender," p. 11.

Suggested Readings

Bonner, Elena. *Mothers and Daughters*. New York: Knopf, 1992.

Buckley, Mary, ed. *Women and Perestroika*. Cambridge: Cambridge University Press, 1992.

Clements, Barbara Evans. *Daughters of Revolution: A History of Women in the USSR*. Arlington Heights, IL: Harlan Davidson, 1994.

Ginzburg, Evgeniia. *Journey into the Whirlwind*. New York: Harcourt Brace, 1967; and *Within the Whirlwind*. New York: Harcourt Brace, 1981.

Glas: *New Russian Writing, No. 3, Women's View*. Sommerville, MA: Zephyr Press, 1992.

Goldman, Wendy. *Women, the State and Revolution*. Cambridge: Cambridge University Press, 1993.

Gorbachev, Raisa. *I Hope: Reminiscences and Reflections*. New York: Harper Collins, 1991.

Goscilo, Helena, ed. *Balancing Acts*. Bloomington: Indiana University Press, 1989.

Gray, Francine du Plessix. *Soviet Women: Walking the Tightrope*. New York: Doubleday, 1989.

Mamonova, Tatyana, ed. *Women and Russia: Feminist Writings from the Soviet Union*. Boston: Beacon, 1984.

Stites, Richard. *The Women's Liberation Movement in Russia: Feminism, Nihilism, and Bolshevism*. 2nd ed. Princeton: Princeton University Press, 1991.

ↀↀ

Religion:

From Official Atheism to Freedom of Choice

Carol Garrard

Tucson, Arizona

Immediately after the failure of the hardline coup attempt against Gorbachev in August 1991, Muscovites used block and tackle to haul down the statue of Felix Dzerzhinsky, founder of the Cheka (forerunner of the KGB), from its lofty place in front of the notorious Lyubyanka prison. CNN carried this dramatic event live, but missed what happened shortly thereafter. Some unknown person painted in large white letters on the empty pedestal the two words, *Sim pobedishi*, the Church Slavic translation of the Latin *In hoc signo vinces—By this sign shalt thou conquer*.

This graffiti proclaims the triumph of Orthodox Christianity over its persecutor, the KGB, and heralds the resurgence of the Russian Orthodox Church. This resurgence is also being felt by other Christian confessions, and by Jews and Muslims. But the majority of the 35 million people in Russia (approximately 40% of the adult population) who consider themselves religious are Orthodox. Their reemergence is the most significant.

(Photo: John Garrard)

An empty plinth, where once stood the bronze visage of Felix Dzerzhinsky, founding father of the Soviet secret police, now proclaims the triumph of Christ over the church's bitterest enemy. The Lubyanka prison, scene of thousands of executions in its cellars during the Stalinist Terror, looms in the background.

The power of the message contained in *by this sign shalt thou conquer* is drawn in part from the parallel between the collapse of the Soviet system and a celebrated turning point in the early history of Christianity. From 302–312 A.D., Christians experienced the "Great Persecution" ordered by the emperor Diocletian. During this time, they were forced either to renounce their faith and make public sacrifices to Rome's pagan gods or be thrown to the lions. In 312 A.D., Constantine saw the Greek monogram for Christ, *Chi* and *Rho*, appear in the heavens. He had the sign painted on his soldiers' shields and won the decisive victory over Maxentius that led to his becoming sole Roman Emperor. In gratitude, he adopted the faith himself and established Christianity as the state religion of Imperial Rome.

In 1991, Boris Yeltsin owed his survival in some measure to a respect for the church. When he stood alone before the tanks and armored personnel carriers assembled by the Party and KGB hardliners, he received only words of sympathy from Western leaders. But upon appealing to the newly installed Patriarch

Aleksii, Yeltsin received immediate help in defeating the coup plotters. In those tense hours on August 19, the Patriarch excommunicated and condemned those who supported the coup. When the KGB ordered its elite SWAT team, the Alpha unit, to storm the Russian Federation building, the men refused. At this critical moment, the coup faltered and soon collapsed. Symbolically, from this moment, the Russian Orthodox religion could begin to recover its patrimony, its churches, and its place in the Russia emerging from the old Soviet Union.

Soviet Persecution of the Orthodox Church

Unlike Diocletian, the Soviet Union did not put Russian Orthodox Christians to the lions. But it did persecute believers as relentlessly and insidiously, and over a much longer period of time. The official "faith" of the USSR was Marxism-Leninism which the Communist Party termed "scientific atheism." The country functioned as if it were a theocracy, only under a secular religion in which the state employed atheist workers to teach scientific atheism in every Soviet school. They did not discriminate between religions—all were persecuted, including Russian Orthodox, the Protestant confessions, Catholicism, Judaism, and Islam. But Russian Orthodoxy received special attention. Having been the state religion of tsarist Russia, it possessed more wealth, more buildings, more clerics, and more believers than any other faith.

There is general agreement that between 1917 and 1923, over 1200 Orthodox priests and 28 bishops were murdered under Lenin's regime. Stalin accelerated the pace of murder, simultaneously ordering the Red Army and enthusiastic Party "shock workers" to seize churches, convents and monasteries. All were robbed of their treasures in icons, many of which were encrusted with jewels and covered with gold and silver, as well as countless other precious items. Some buildings were destroyed, including the huge Cathedral of Christ the Savior, forty-five years in construction, in Moscow in 1931. The vast empty space was turned into an open-air swimming pool, after the ground failed to bear the weight of a gigantic monument to Lenin. Other churches were seized and put to secular use, typically as warehouses, but also for office space. Monasteries in outlying areas, and especially in the far north, were taken over by the secret police and used as prisons. By the late 1930s, only about sixty monasteries remained functioning out of more than a thousand that had existed before 1917.

War Comes to the Rescue

If the early pace of destruction, appropriation and murder had continued, it is questionable whether the Orthodox Church could have survived. There was no Patriarch and the Church hierarchy never met. Ironically, it was Hitler's invasion of the Soviet Union in June 1941 that saved the Orthodox Church from complete annihilation. Realizing that the Russian people would not fight to save either him or his brutal regime, Stalin turned the war into a struggle between Holy Russia and her eternal foe, the Teutons. He permitted the Church to reemerge, to bless the departing troops,

"The Banishment from the Cloister," a lithograph by the well-known Russian artist Tatiana Kiselyova, depicts the closing of the Seraphim-Diveyevo nunnery in 1933 under Stalin. Tatiana Kiselyova is a member of the congregation of St. Vladimir's Russian Orthodox Church in Moscow.

to proclaim Hitler the anti-Christ, and to collect funds for the war effort.

On September 4, 1943—when final victory was no longer in doubt after the triumphs at Stalingrad and Kursk—Stalin summoned three metropolitans (bishops ranking below the Patriarch, each controlling an ecclesiastical province) for one of his notorious midnight meetings at the Kremlin. He agreed to their request that Orthodoxy's ecclesiastical council, or *Synod*, be reassembled (it had not existed since 1935) and a *Sobor* (an official assembly) be held to elect a new Patriarch. Stalin joked about the need to employ "Bolshevik drive" to get the *Sobor* held quickly. In reality, Stalin and his advisors had already decided who should win the election. It took place in only four days. On September 8, the new Orthodox Church hierarchy was flown in by Soviet military aircraft.

A Devil's Bargain

The new Patriarch Sergei, Metropolitan of Moscow and acting Patriarch since 1937, was offered the famous Novodevichy Monastery as his headquarters, and he was provided with a car and other material comforts. Religious activities were monitored by a new Council on Orthodox Church Affairs, but the Church was permitted to re-open some seminaries and monasteries, to publish a small number of Bibles for sale to the public (between 1917 and 1943 no Orthodox Bibles were printed in the Soviet Union), and to worship in controlled conditions in designated "prayer buildings" at the pleasure of the state. The Russian Orthodox Church thus survived, but at a heavy price.

In the postwar years, the Soviet regime coerced the Church more harshly, particularly under Nikita Khrushchev, who ordered a new wave of destruction and arrests of priests. Under Brezhnev the Party used the KGB to infiltrate both congregations and the priesthood. Until the end of the Soviet period, religious activity was carefully circumscribed and controlled, not only by the 1929 law on religious associations, but by a number of Party directives that were classic Catch-22s.

The state did not recognize the Russian Orthodox Church or any other church as a single entity. Instead it permitted believers to organize only separate *associations* or *societies*. The Soviet Constitution of 1936 declared that the purpose of such associations was to "perform religious rites and hold prayer meetings and ceremonies together for the purposes of worship." However, teaching, preaching or proselytizing were strictly forbidden. Article 52 of the 1977 Soviet Constitution guaranteed each citizen "the right to profess any religion or to profess none, to celebrate religious rites, or to conduct atheist propaganda." Further, the statute banned religious education. It was not against the law to be a believer, but teaching children, gaining converts, doing charity, selling religious materials, etc. was forbidden. The Bible itself was generally unavailable, and Soviet customs officials did all they could to prevent foreigners from attempting to smuggle them into the country. Copying religious materials was very difficult, because all copy machines belonged to the state, and access to them was severely restricted. The authorities were particularly vigilant in preventing copying of religious materials for children.

The Soviet legal code prescribed stringent penalties—up to five years in prison—for those who dared to "encroach on the rights of their fellow citizens under the guise of performing religious rites." That offense in the penal code was listed along with "maintaining dens of depravity" and "preparation and distribution of pornographic material." In short, the penal code took Marx's metaphor that *religion is the opiate of the masses* and translated it into statutes and laws.

In order to worship legally, a congregation had to become an officially registered religious association and provide its own prayer building. This was the first of the exquisite tortures applied to religious believers. There were no churches available, since almost all had been commandeered by the atheist state. The proviso that a congregation already had to have a prayer building before even applying for registration was designed to cut off the process before it got started. Furthermore, conducting religious rites in the open air or in people's homes was also illegal. As a consequence, some Russian Orthodox believers went underground, just as the early Christians under Nero and Diocletian had done.

One illustration of the dangers believers faced is told in the story of Father Sergii, a middle-aged priest with a noble face and a luxurious black beard, and his congregation of St. Vladimir's Church In Moscow. [1] Without an approved prayer building, Father Sergii conducted discussion seminars for adults in people's apartments. Often, people crowded into the small Soviet apartments so tightly that they could hardly breathe or find space to stand. Father Sergii also secretly taught the catechism to children. In the 1980s, he had older children prepare reports on various religious themes. For holidays in the Orthodox calendar, Father Sergii had the children prepare plays to re-enact Bible stories. This included writing a script, making scenery and costumes, learning lines, having dress rehearsals, and finally performing in a cramped Moscow apartment in front of proud parents.

As one of the mothers recalled: "After the play, we enjoyed a feast of all the special foods that are traditional for these holidays." This was the Russian version of a church potluck supper, but at the time the element of danger was always present. This same woman continued:

> We always knew that at any minute there could be a ring at the door and people could burst in and disrupt our activities. The great majority of us were prepared morally for whatever would take place. Thanks be to the Lord that we did not suffer, although Father Sergii himself did undergo persecution. He was summoned on a number of occasions by the authorities, who warned him that he should cease his religious activities. Letters denouncing him were written. He was accused of holding evening services and of having connections with dissidents.

The inference is clear. They were betrayed by someone from within the congregation.

Agents in Cassocks

This betrayal by one or more placed within their midst exemplifies the cruelest blow the Party struck at the Orthodox Church: penetration by KGB agents or informers. During the Brezhnev era, the Party increasingly relied upon this strategy, codenamed "Z."

"Z" was a special directorate of the KGB charged with monitoring church activities. It proved remarkably imaginative. Congregations were infiltrated. Priests were offered the devil's bargain of either collaborating with the state or facing the Gulag. The hierarchy was riddled with "agents in cassocks."

People could be compromised and threatened with public exposure. They could be bribed with money, scarce consumer goods, or permission to travel abroad. Any activity performed with foreign church delegations was always controlled by KGB officers. Until the election of Aleksii Ridiger of Leningrad (now St. Petersburg) to the position of Patriarch on June 6, 1990, nominations to the position of Patriarch were cleared by the KGB.

During this time, the Patriarchate went to almost any length to placate the Party, as the trials of Father Sergii illustrate. When he resisted attempts to compromise his role as a priest, the authorities took action against him. He was forced to leave Moscow in 1980 and was transferred by an obliging Orthodox Church hierarchy to a distant, small church. This meant Father Sergii had a "place of worship" but it was far removed from his congregation. Irina, a singer in the choir, explained the rationale without bitterness, accepting the Church's compromised position as a reality, part of the price they paid to be able to worship at all:

> It was done so that we would be deprived of his leadership. These were very difficult years for all of us. Nevertheless, though we had to travel a long distance to get to the church to which Father Sergii had been transferred, and though the church was very tiny and we were very cramped, we went.

When the coup's collapse in August 1991 led to "Z" being abolished, the archives of the Church Department were opened to a commission, and informers and agents were publicly unmasked. The information from the "Z" files was dismaying. In January, 1992, three Orthodox priests published information from the archives alleging that two permanent members of the Church's ruling *Holy Synod* and the head of its Publications Department were KGB informants.

The Turnaround Under *Glasnost'*

One of the small victories the Church achieved on the one-thousandth anniversary of Russia's acceptance of Christianity was Father Sergii's return to Moscow in 1988. His next step was to get a prayer building in the city. The Russian Orthodox Church petitioned the Moscow City Council to get the Church of St. Vladimir returned. Although Father Sergii and his congregation found that though they had won this skirmish, they were far from winning the war. Father Sergii explained:

> It took more than a year to get the official transfer of the church on paper, and then physically to occupy the church building. The church was being used as a book depository by the state historical library. There was nowhere to move the books, so the people who worked there refused to leave.

Help came from an unexpected quarter. The head of the local unit of Moscow Power and Light stopped by and told Father Sergii that he himself was a believer and would see what he could do.

The man was as good as his word. He simply had the gas and electricity cut off from the church building. After a week in the cold and dark, the book depository's workers were ready to strike a deal. The church had already been physically divided into two halves by the Soviet authorities. Therefore, the state bureaucrats vacated the half with the cupola, pushing and shoving the books into the other half of the building. Whatever cataloguing system had been used prior to the forced commingling was shelved as well, as the books were wedged in from floor to ceiling.

At least the depository staff did not have to worry about disappointing disgruntled readers, for these books had never circulated, nor indeed, have they been seen since 1945. Here sits what is referred to by locals as "Hitler's library." Father Sergii explained: *These books belong to the Third Reich, and perhaps some of them did come from Hitler's Chancellery. Our army brought them back from Berlin after the Nazis surrendered.* Behind barred windows, rats can be seen scurrying up and down stacked columns of leather bindings, chewing their priceless vellum. The German government is aware of the books, but no agreement has thus far been reached for their return to Berlin.

When Father Sergii and his congregation occupied their half of the church building, they had the immense job of cleaning and restoration. Like all Orthodox churches commandeered by the Soviet state, St. Vladimir's had been "renovated" for secular purposes. Three floors, each floor containing rooms, walls, ceilings and electrical fixtures, had been built into it. All of this had to be torn down. In just a few months, Father Sergii's congregation restored their half to the point where once again services could be sung beneath the onion dome.

The work of restoration is ongoing. New recruits swell the ranks continually. Father Sergii has been able to attract many volunteers. Not all attend services or join the congregation. They seem instead to feel good just by helping. "Sweat equity" substitutes for money, although Father Sergii explained that he is obliged to hire professional workers to do technical repairs and install heating and water pipes. The church's proximity to several institutes and colleges has meant that a large pool of young

(Photo: John Garrard)

The Russian Orthodox Church of St. Vladimir's, an eighteenth century building restored by the congregation, is only a few miles from the Kremlin. In the back half of the building, the "Library of the Third Reich," which was brought back from Berlin by the Red Army in 1945, is warehoused.

people are nearby. Many have been attracted by the energetic restoration going on in their midst and have come over to watch, sometimes asking Father Sergii if they may help.

The progress made by the congregation at St. Vladimir's is all the more remarkable since they, like virtually all Orthodox congregations, are essentially penniless. The churches in Soviet times were subject to numerous financial restrictions and inequities. One of the most notorious was the sale of religious artifacts to foreigners, including America's own Ambassador Joseph Davies in the 1930s. Stalin's government permitted Davies to purchase national treasures at ridiculously low prices, and in return Davies supplied the Western media with good copy about the dictator and his regime, notably in the unintentional comedy, *Mission to Moscow*. Other Western governments and officials participated in the Soviet fire sale of Orthodoxy's treasures. In 1933, the regime sold one of the three most valuable complete Bible texts in existence, the *Codex Sinaiticus*, to the British Museum for half a million dollars. This *Codex* is the sole copy of the *Greek New Testament* in uncial letters. It was given in 1859 to the tsar for safekeeping by the monks of St. Catherine's Monastery, a sixth-century Greek Orthodox monastery in the Sinai desert. Such plundering of antiquities during Stalin's time bankrupted the Russian Orthodox Church, not only of its finances, but many of its irreplaceable cultural artifacts.

Restoring a church in less than a year with no budget was not the only challenge accepted by the congregation of St. Vladimir's. They further extended their focus to the nearby Cathedral of St. John the Baptist. The Cathedral is still fully occupied by the Ministry of Internal Affairs, or MVD (the regular police, roughly equivalent to America's FBI), who use it as their national training academy. It would seem to be an impossible objective, not unlike having a religious group in the United States wanting to take over the FBI's training facilities in Quantico, Virginia. However, it may not be impossible. Friendly relations with the commanding general of the MVD academy have already been established with the congregation of St. Vladimir's. When Father Sergii petitioned the Moscow City Council to hold a religious procession around the

(Photo: John Garrard)

A student from the nearby university inquired of Father Sergii, "Are you with the church?" He then volunteered, "I want to help." This young man was shortly seen assisting in the restoration work—his first task was to dig out old sewer lines!

cathedral building on the liturgical calendar's feast day of St. John the Baptist, permission was granted. Father Sergii dressed in his robes and led a procession of children singing and chanting around the outside of the building. As he swung the censer, and sprinkled the holy water, the doors to the cathedral itself opened. Father Sergii led his tiny pilgrimage through the enormous building, now used as a cafeteria, printing shop, offices, firing range, and classrooms. Some of the MVD officers jeered, but others did not, as an eyewitness recounted:

> Suddenly some of the men rushed over to Father Sergii. They threw themselves at his feet, and tears streamed down their faces. They held up their hands, and beseeched him, saying "Sprinkle me with the Holy water too, Father. Bless me too, for I have sinned."

The struggle between St. Vladimir's and the MVD Academy over the Cathedral may not be as disproportionate as it seemed at first.

"Man Does Not Live by Bread Alone"

In the midst of crippling inflation and a shattered economy, the loyal parishioners of St. Vladimir's believe the present is a comparative paradise. One of the parents at St. Vladimir's Elementary School said:

> Many problems lie ahead, but it is a miracle what we have achieved already in less than a year. Now our children can study God's word, and they can pray together, both before and after meals, before their classes, and can sing hymns and go to church on Sundays with their parents, all together in one church.

For people in the West, where freedom of religion is assumed as a constitutional liberty, such joy may seem difficult to understand. But there was no missing the intensity of feelings among the believers, nor the courage required to persevere in their faith:

> Two years ago when we prayed together, or sang hymns, or studied the Bible, it was all done in secret. Even just two years ago, our children had to be careful about wearing a cross around their neck. They were studying in Soviet schools and were subject to attacks by aggressively atheist students, and worst of all, teachers.

There are extreme contrasts in reemerging Russia. One very marked contrast is between the gentle behavior of some of the

(Photo: John Garrard)

The Cathedral of St. John the Baptist is located inside the high walls of the Ivanovsky Convent. The Cathedral is an enormous complex, built in the 19th century, and today is occupied by the Russian MVD, the equivalent of America's FBI.

parishioners at St. Vladimir's and others who seethe with understandable anger and frustration on Moscow's dilapidated streets. Walking out of a nearly empty dairy store, a woman deliberately bangs the door in the face of the next customer. Too often Russian faces seem like fists, tightened with the strain of running the gauntlet of nearly bare shops to find food to put on the table. Members of Father Sergii's congregation seem not to have anger and despair stamped on their countenances. Their expressions are optimistic and purposeful, in spite of the great problems they face. Nevertheless, their daunting task of spiritual and moral reeducation of a congregation will require every bit of hope and inner strength they can command.

Old Habits or a New LEAF

The future of Russian Orthodoxy is clouded. While Russians now enjoy freedom to worship in public, no one can be sure how they will use this freedom politically. The old Orthodox church was linked with tsarist traditions, not to political democracy. Some members of the Orthodox Church hierarchy who cooperated with the Party and the KGB in the past still hold their posts. Other Russians who belong to anti-Semitic and reactionary ultra-nationalist organizations want Orthodoxy to become once again the center of a nationalistic, anti-Western reactionary movement. Orthodoxy's revival may well bring back an intolerance of Western Christianities, and of Judaism and Islam, as well.

The historical precedent is grim, for the old Orthodox church, although powerful, was never independent. When Russian Orthodoxy was the established Church of Russia, it was a compliant ally of the tsars. For most of its history, it was a prop to Russian autocracy. By the early 1500s, Moscow was destined to become the queen of Christendom. Rome had fallen to the "Latin heresy"—Catholicism—and Constantinople, the Second Rome, had fallen to the Muslim Turks. The monk Filofey is noted for the zealous phrase: *Two Romes have fallen, but the third [Moscow] stands, and a fourth shall not be.* This historical zealousness provokes the question: What is the brooding power of Christianity that lies waiting to emerge in Russia today?

Fortunately, recent surveys show that Orthodox believers, even those described as "fervent," do not hold extremist views. Religious believers cannot be lumped into any particular political basket. Many believers, especially those in Moscow and St. Petersburg, profess liberal views. This may be the result of a combination of educated, women believers: two-thirds of believers in these two cities are women, fewer than half (42%) are aged fifty or more, and 29% have a higher education. Religious belief in Russia today is contrary to what statistics typically indicate. Generally, religious belief increases with age and is also higher among the less educated. It is significant that nearly 30% of Russian female believers have higher education, a slightly higher statistic than for

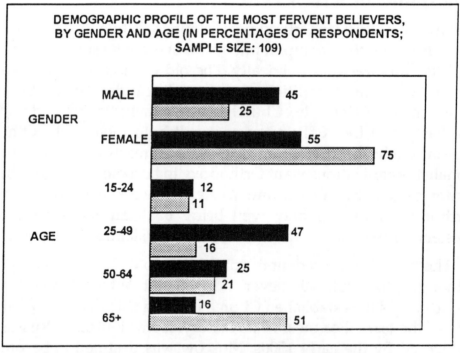

The chart shows that the most fervent believers are largely older women. But much of the energy of the Russian Orthodox revival is being fueled by young people, who first come to aid in church restoration as a way to recapture their heritage, but then sometimes stay as part of the congregation. (Mark Rhodes, "Diversity of Political Views among Russia's Believers," RFE/RL Research Report, Vol. 3, No. 11. March 18, 1994, p. 46.)

their male counterparts. Since it is women who are taking a leading role in bringing Russians back to the church—just as many of Jesus' early followers were women—this can be interpreted with some hope.

We in the West should pay careful heed to what is happening to religions in Russia. When Christianity split into its Eastern and Western halves in 1054, the fault line ran down through what became Yugoslavia. Ethnically, these people were identical: they were all Southern Slavs. But today, fighting continues between the Serbs, who are Orthodox, and the Croats, who are Catholic. Serbs and Croats find one common ground: a shared willingness to kill their Muslim neighbors. They contemptuously dismiss Muslims as "Turks", since these people are descendants of converts to Islam under the 500 year rule of the Ottoman Empire. As we gaze in disbelief at the fratricidal bloodshed of what is largely a religious war in Bosnia, we should be aware that should Russian Orthodoxy go the way of Serbian Orthodoxy, the world will have a far more dangerous problem on its hands. Religious-based politics have written the text of many nation's histories and are the subject of present-day headlines. This is not something to be ignored.

During this time of great upheaval and search for identity, it is in everyone's interest to celebrate the freedom of worship in reemerging Russia in ways that do not incite traditional and nationalist suspicions in Russia or in the West. In its search for religious identity, the Russia of today faces many dilemmas. It can reinstate attitudes of intolerance from the past. Or it can create a new future by embracing the essence of freedom—the simple ability to be able to choose.

Endnote

[1]My contact with Father Sergii and his congregation resulted from acting as a courier for citizens of Tucson, Arizona. For two humanitarian missions, parishioners of Our Savior's Lutheran Church, students at Sunrise Elementary School, and many local doctors donated over twenty crates of badly needed medicines and supplies to this church. The identification of Father Sergii's congregation resulted from an initiative by Roger and Joyce Stewart, Tucson philanthropists and industrialists. The children of Sunrise Elemen-

tary School, led by the resource specialist Mrs. Mimi Crowley, still continue a lively exchange of pen pal letters and gifts with their Russian friends.

Suggested Readings

Armes, Keith. "Russian Patriarch and Communist Caesar," in *Religious Life in Russia*. Boston: Boston University Institute for the Study of Conflict, Ideology and Policy, 1992.

Billington, James H. *Russia Transformed: Breakthrough to Hope*. New York: Free Press, 1992.

Bourdeaux, Michael. *The Gospel's Triumph Over Communism*. Minneapolis, MN: Bethany House, 1991.

Fletcher, William. *A Study in Survival: The Church in Russia, 1927–1943*. New York: MacMillan, 1965.

Curtiss, John Shelton. *The Russian Church and the Soviet State, 1917–1950*. New York: Little, Brown, 1953.

Elliott, Mark. "For Christian Understanding, Ignorance is Not Bliss," in *East-West Church and Ministry Report*. No. 1. Wheaton, IL: Wheaton College, Summer, 1993, pp. 7–8.

Ellis, Jane. *The Russian Orthodox Church*. Bloomington: Indiana University Press, 1986.

Hill, Kent R. "The Orthodox Church and a Pluralistic Society," in *Russian Pluralism, Now Irreversible?*, ed. Uri Ra'anan, Keith Armes, and Kate Martin. New York: St. Martin's, 1992, pp. 165–188.

Kishkovsky, Leonid. "The Mission of the Russian Orthodox Church After Communism," in *East-West Church and Ministry Report*, Wheaton, IL: Wheaton College, No. 1 Summer 1993, pp. 1–2.

Pospielovsky, Dimitry. *The Russian Church Under the Soviet Regime, 1917-1982*, 2 Vols. Crestwood, NY: St. Vladimir's Seminary Press, 1984.

Rhodes, Mark. "Diversity of Political Views among Russia's Believers," *RFE/RL Research Report*. Munich, Germany: Radio Liberty Research, Vol. 3, No. 11. March 18, 1994, pp. 44–50.

Steeves, Paul, ed. *The Modern Encyclopedia of Religions in Russia and the Soviet Union*. Gulf Breeze, FL: Academic International Press, 1988.

Empire and Nation:

Cultural Diversity in the Russian Federation

Stephen K. Batalden

Arizona State University, Phoenix, Arizona

In 1829, a young Russian intellectual created an uproar simply by asking what it meant to be a Russian. Peter Chaadaev, in his "Philosophical Letters," criticized Russian culture for lacking the "unity of vision" found in the West:

> To look at us, one might come to believe that the general law of mankind has been revoked in our case. We are alone in the world, we have given nothing to the world, we have taught it nothing. We have not added a single idea to the sum total of human ideas. . . . While the entire world was rebuilding itself, we constructed nothing, but went on squatting in our thatched huts. . . . The new destinies of the human race were not for us.[1]

Chaadaev asked whether Russia had something unique to offer, or whether it should simply imitate the achievements of the West. He concluded: *We must repeat for ourselves the education of the human race.* Chaadaev argued that Russian culture was backward and needed to turn to Western moral and religious traditions.

The questions raised in Chaadaev's letters were to become central to the ongoing search for a Russian national identity: Where is Russia going? Does it have its own authentic past? Does it have a unique mission for the future? Central to the debate in 1829 was the question of Russia's relationship to the West.

Today, a century and a half later, the collapse of the Soviet Union and the sudden loss of territories once part of the Russian Empire pose questions comparable to those raised by Chaadaev. Where is Russia going? What is the meaning of its past, and what is its role in the world? Is it Russia's fate simply to imitate the nations of Western Europe?

There is one critical difference today. In Chaadaev's time, the stability and unity of the Russian Empire under Tsar Nicholas I went largely unchallenged and the empire continued to grow. The government assumed that newly acquired regions would readily become integrated into the Russian Empire. Today, that integration is lacking. Instead, the Russian nation is only one part of a culturally diverse Russian Federation that used to be linked to fourteen other Soviet republics in an empire that has now collapsed. The question being asked in Russia is whether or not the complex ethnic and cultural, economic, environmental, and political differences can be woven together to create a fabric that accentuates both individual and collective identities?

According to the 1989 census, out of a total population of about 147 million, there are approximately 120 million Russians in the Russian Federation. There are sizable minorities everywhere. From the small indigenous nations of the Russian north, such as the Chukchi, Dolgans, Nentsy, Eskimos, Evenks, and Evens, to the Dagestanis, Chechens, and Ingushy of the Russian Caucasus, and east to the Buriat Mongols beyond Lake Baikal, the Russian Federation is a country of overwhelming cultural and ethnic diversity. With the collapse of the USSR, many of these ancient geographic homelands have become the focus of awakened ethnic identity. Russians now seek their national identity in a Federation marked by heightened ethnic, cultural, and regional diversity.

Some Russians are dissatisfied. In 1994, Vladimir Zhirinovsky, a Russian right-wing political leader and head of the misnamed Liberal Democratic Party, demanded the recovery of Russia's nineteenth-century imperial borders from Finland to Alaska.

What Zhirinovsky did not clarify was how he would forge a homogeneous empire from the cultural and ethnic diversity of Eurasia.

At the other end of the ethnic and political spectrum, there are ethnic secessionists who have attempted to establish sovereign states within the Russian Federation, or who have declared independence and tried to abandon the Federation altogether. Most notable have been the self-proclaimed independent Republic of Tatarstan, far to the east of Moscow, and the Republic of Chechenia, located in the northern Caucasus region. Both are rich in natural resources. Such unchecked regional and ethnic splintering cannot be discounted entirely given the lingering political instability in Moscow.

Between these extremes of forcibly restored imperial grandeur on the one hand, and anarchic breakaway regions on the other, Russian society and its leaders are struggling with the problem of how a reemerging Russia should respond to its internal diversity, to Russian traditions, and to the West.

Center and Periphery: Defining the New Federalism

As the official name "Russian Federation" indicates, in the wake of the collapse of the Union of Soviet Socialist Republics (USSR), policymakers in Moscow have sought federative solutions. In practice, this has meant making concessions to local regions or leaders in an effort to hold the Federation together. The idea of a federation is not new. The United States was born a federation and so was the USSR. The former Russian Soviet Federated Socialist Republic (RSFSR) was established in 1918 as the largest of what became fifteen union republics within the USSR. However, neither the USSR nor the RSFSR ever functioned as a true federation. Under Lenin, Stalin, and their successors, the autonomy of the regions was strictly subordinate to the powers in Moscow.

There have been additional complications to the establishment of a new federation. Frequently there are more Russians than there are members of the local nationality in the ethnic homelands. For example, there are many more Russians than Mordvins

European Russia

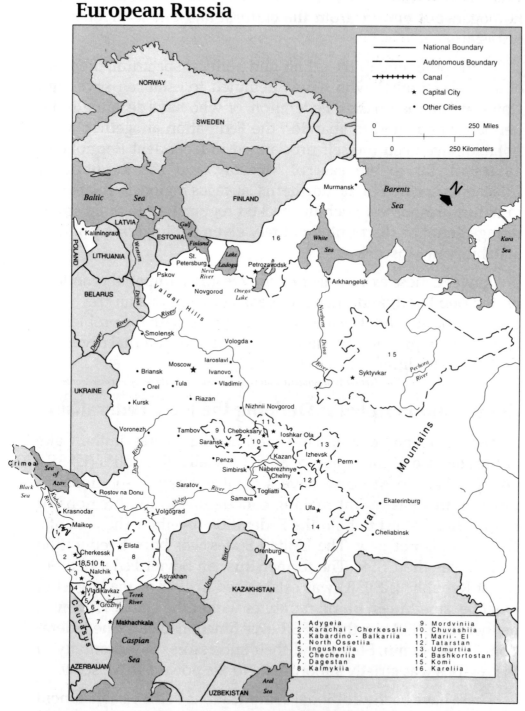

	National Boundary
	Autonomous Boundary
┼┼┼┼┼	Canal
★	Capital City
•	Other Cities

1. Adygeia
2. Karachai - Cherkessiia
3. Kabardino - Balkariia
4. North Ossetiia
5. Ingushetiia
6. Checheniia
7. Dagestan
8. Kalmykiia
9. Mordviniia
10. Chuvashiia
11. Marii - El
12. Tatarstan
13. Udmurtiia
14. Bashkortostan
15. Komi
16. Kareliia

Reprinted from *The Newly Independent States of Eurasia: Handbook of Former Soviet Republics* by Stephen K. Batalden and Sandra L. Batalden, with permission from The Oryx Press, 4041 N. Central at Indian School Rd., Phoenix, AZ 85012, (800) 279-ORYX.

in Mordviniia, and many more Russians than Buriats in Buriatiia. In heavily populated Tatarstan, there are only slightly more Tatars than Russians. The chart below indicates a sample of the percentages of Russians and those nationalities for which the regions are named, as well as total population:

**Selected Russian Republics: Total Population with Percentages
of Titular Nationality and Russians**

Buriatiia	1,038,000
Buriats	24.0%
Russians	69.9%
Mordviniia	964,000
Mordvins	32.5%
Russians	60.8%
Sakha (Iakutiia)	1,094,000
Iakuts	33.4%
Russians	50.3%
Tatarstan	3,642,000
Tatars	48.5%
Russians	43.3%

Reprinted from *The Newly Independent States of Eurasia: Handbook of Former Soviet Republics* by Stephen K. Batalden and Sandra L. Batalden, with permission from The Oryx Press, 4041 N. Central at Indian School Rd., Phoenix, AZ 85012, (800) 279-ORYX.

In March 1992, Russian Federation President Boris Yeltsin signed a federal treaty with most of Russia's autonomous republics and regions. It provided that the land and natural resources of the republics belonged to their inhabitants. In theory, this meant that, for example, the diamonds of the Sakha [Iakut] Republic in Russian Siberia, once controlled by Moscow, would now be regulated by the local republic. In practice, however, the terms of ownership over such natural resources were never clarified.

In the parliamentary elections of December 1993, voters of the Russian Federation narrowly approved a new constitution. Central to that constitution is the establishment of a two-house parliament. The upper chamber or "Senate" provides equal representation for all autonomous units of the Russian Federation in the same way that the U.S. Senate equally represents the fifty states. But the new constitution fails to spell out precisely the division of

Russian Federation

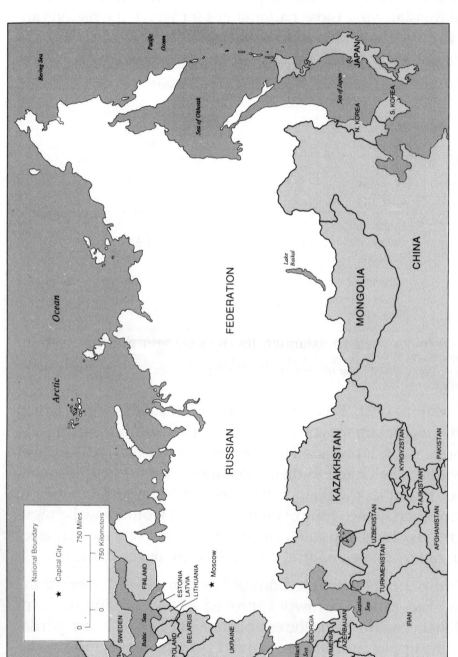

Reprinted from *The Newly Independent States of Eurasia: Handbook of Former Soviet Republics* by Stephen K. Batalden and Sandra L. Batalden, with permission from The Oryx Press, 4041 N. Central at Indian School Rd., Phoenix, AZ 85012, (800) 279-ORYX.

authority between the center and the peripheral regions. Some provisions clearly describe the rights of the central government. Other provisions describe cases in which the central and regional institutions share authority, such as in health care and education. However, the new Russian constitution is vague in the assignment of powers to constituent republics and regions, powers that Americans associate with their "federal system."

The Case of Tatarstan

An interesting test case is the Republic of Tatarstan. Tatarstan is located on the upper Volga River. In February 1994, a treaty was signed between Russia and Tatarstan.[3] The treaty did not recognize Tatarstan's independence, as many Tatars had demanded. It did, however, grant more privileges to Tatarstan than those guaranteed other republics. Here are some examples: 1) Tatarstan was given the right to determine who is a citizen; 2) it was given the right to exempt its citizens from Russian military service; 3) it's right to conduct its own foreign policy and trade was recognized; 4) it was permitted to establish its own budget and tax system; and 5) it was given the right to administer its own natural resources. However, the treaty called for a future joint agreement on oil production, an issue crucial to Russian economic stability.

This "Treaty of Delimitation" signaled a temporary resolution to the impasse between Russian central authority and this comparatively wealthy and potentially independent republic. But the Russia-Tatarstan agreement failed to satisfy all parties. Russia's ardent nationalists reject such treaties with subject peoples. Some Tatar nationalists, on the other hand, see the document as sacrificing too much sovereignty. Under such tensions, the future of the multi-national Russian Federation continues to be hammered out.

The Case of the Siberian North

Unlike Tatarstan, the Siberian far north is inhabited by a much smaller percentage of indigenous non-Russian population. Yet, as in the case of Tatarstan, the issues of economic development and the control of natural resources are most important.

Siberia and the Far East

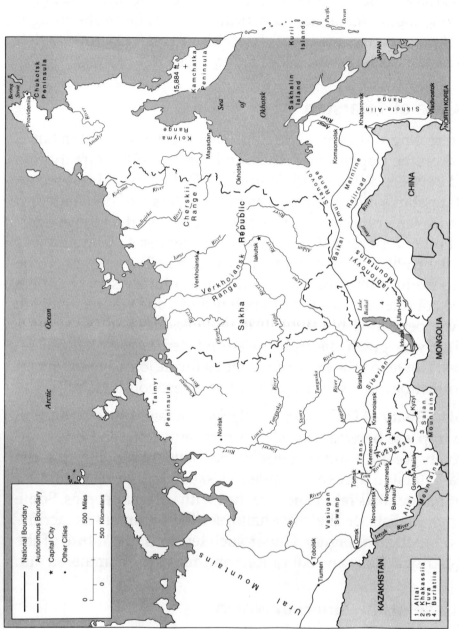

Reprinted from *The Newly Independent States of Eurasia: Handbook of Former Soviet Republics* by Stephen K. Batalden and Sandra L. Batalden, with permission from The Oryx Press, 4041 N. Central at Indian School Rd., Phoenix, AZ 85012, (800) 279-ORYX.

Seventy years ago, after the Revolution, the new Soviet Union had to decide how Siberia would be ruled. In 1924, a "Committee for Assisting the Peoples of the Far North" was established. Its governmental officials and scholars debated the best approach toward Siberian development. Conservative members of the committee sought to give high priority to protecting the ecology and the status of numerous indigenous people. Progressive members believed that the task of the committee was to open up development of the enormous natural and mineral resources of the Siberian north.

By the end of the 1920s, the progressive members had won. The idea of national autonomy for local indigenous peoples of the north—some of them very closely related to American Eskimos—was secondary to the rapid industrial development of the region. It did not take long for Soviet collective farms and industrialization to transform the nomadic communities of northern herders into fixed settlements tied directly to Soviet control. "Red Tents" or Soviet cultural bases were established where local children were raised in isolation from their families. Thus, Soviet control introduced formal schooling and mass literacy to the local population, but undermined the traditional cultures and languages of the non-Russian people of Siberia in the process.

From the 1950s, this Russian Sovietization of Siberia was particularly aggressive. The north was *not so much developed as conquered.*[4] The results have been devastating to the fragile environment of the frozen northern tundra. This "conquest" was equally threatening to the small nations of the north: their nomadic fishing and herding customs, their oral traditions, their tribal councils, and their native languages.

Today, the indigenous peoples of the Russian far north, like their Alaskan Eskimo cousins across the Bering Straits, face common problems of preserving minority cultural and linguistic identities. This sense of shared Siberian and Alaskan cultural inheritance has been captured by Yevgeny Yevtushenko, a modern Russian poet. Yevtushenko visited Alaska on a poetry-reading tour in 1966, was impressed with the cultural unity of the native peoples of Siberia and Alaska, separated by politics during the

Cold War. The result was a wonderful book of photographs and verse that described the arctic sable as one of few creatures that could freely roam between two identical northern lands:

> *Beyond the silently sleeping*
> *strip of water*
> *an American soldier*
> *listens and hears. . . .*
> *And the sable, the sable,*
> *with special tread*
> *circles on the ice floes in the bay,*
> *tail puffed up,*
> *between two systems,*
> *and chrysanthemum floes,*
> *between two radars,*
> *between two blows*
> *running from ice to ice*
> *without a tremble. . .*[5]

The relationship between the Russian majority and the indigenous minorities of Tatarstan and Siberia illustrates some of the problems of the Russian Federation as a whole. Under what terms is the cultural diversity of the Russian Federation sustainable? Industrial development, while serving the short-term interests of the majority and minority alike, threatens the long-term cultural survival of vulnerable non-Russians. Much like the protection of endangered biological species, the protection of cultural diversity in the Russian Federation is an exceedingly complex matter.

Today growing coalitions of Russian environmentalists and activists concerned with human rights are opposing unregulated economic development of their regions. But no industrial development means no jobs and the possibility of an even greater economic crisis which would be felt by Russians and non-Russians alike. A case in point is timber cutting in the rich coniferous forest regions of the Siberian taiga. The Siberian taiga holds the largest oxygen-rich coniferous zone in the world. In the context of the current Russian economic crisis, can one question those who would eke out profit by exploiting these natural resources? The fragile arctic delta regions have been the traditional grazing areas for the reindeer herds of endangered indigenous nations. These same deltas contain oil reserves. In a debate reminiscent of that over the Alaskan pipeline a generation ago, environmentalists and minority spokesmen have united to argue for the curtailment of oil drilling in those deltas. The problem is complicated by the possibility that, for a profit, foreigners seek to help the Russians extract that oil and natural gas. Thus not only right-wing Russian nationalist politicians, but also ecologists and native Siberian activists are confronting cultural diversity in the Russian Federation.

When Chaadaev wrote his philosophical letters in the age of the European industrial revolution, he thought that Russia needed only to draw upon the universally applicable cultural and economic achievements of the West. There are those today who argue that privatization, democratization and free markets are what Russia needs. Yet, privatization and democratization, since they would give a voice to the regional and cultural diversity of the Russian Federation, could pose a threat to political stability. Already ravaged by Soviet industrial practices, non-Russian minorities confront a free market that promises to raise living standards at the cost of native ethnic identity.

According to Nikolai T. Yakouba, general director of Russian Far East and Siberian Trade for JK International, an American timber company, the dilemma is as follows:

> We want to do it right. But we can't exactly go in and construct American standard safeguards when competitors are doing things at a third of the price. And we can't be a timber company and stay out of the biggest market on earth. So tell me, how would you protect Siberia?[6]

There are no simple answers. The question of how to find balance in solving this precarious dilemma is as complex as Russia's cultural and ethnic identity.

Russia and the Non-Russian *Other*

No discussion of the Russian nation would be complete without a word about the shock suffered by Russians over the loss of their wider empire. For almost five-hundred years, the Muscovite,

Russian, and Soviet empires dominated Eurasia. This land mass stretched from Poland to the Pacific. It had been inhabited by scores of diverse peoples, each with its own unique past, language, and culture that had existed long before Russian control. In the twentieth-century Soviet Union, this diversity was artificially downplayed. Major nationalities were given Republic status, but Soviet culture, Soviet state economic policy, and the Russian language provided an appearance of unity. Then it all collapsed.

In 1991, in an article in the *New York Times,* Edward Keenan described the Soviet Union as a badly worn linoleum floor, beneath the veneer of which there began to resurface the old wooden floor boards of enduring non-Russian cultures.[7] Suddenly Russians had to redefine themselves not only in terms of the West, but in relation to the lands and peoples of their former empire. For generations, Russians had assumed that all the people in the Soviet Republics were destined to become more and more like Russians. Instead, they became the newly independent states of the *near abroad*—the fourteen new republics created when the USSR collapsed.

In previous centuries, Russians had developed a special vocabulary for reference to these non-Russians. Those outside the Empire were called *inostrantsy*— *foreigners, those from another country.* Non-Russians living *within* the Empire, particularly Tatar and other Turkic peoples, the Finnic peoples of the north, the Buriat Mongols, and even Russia's Jewish population came to be referred as *inorodtsy—those of other birth.* Many of these inorodtsy, because of their Islamic, Jewish, Shamanist, Buddhist or other religious beliefs, were also referred to as i*novertsy—those of other belief.* This distinction between Russians and the others of the empire was one of the hallmarks of the imperial experience.

Although the new Russia of the 1990s retains approximately three-quarters of the lands of the former Soviet Union, the dismemberment of Russia's former imperial holdings has left complicated, unresolved problems and tensions. Using the language of the nineteenth century, millions of the *inorodtsy* have now become *inostrantsy,* foreigners to Russia. Russian settlers and military personnel in these now adjoining but non-Russian states have suddenly become the *other* in lands they controlled for decades. The result has been a fundamental psychological readjustment for Russians at home and abroad. The new relations between Russia and the non-Russians of the *near abroad* have produced self-examination, anxiety, and tensions. Mixed marriages, for example, were on the increase in the late Soviet Union. One legacy is family crisis in an era of renewed nationalism, both in Russia and in the *near abroad.*

What Interest Does Russia Have in the *Near Abroad?*

Given centuries of Russian imperial rule, it is not surprising that the dismemberment of this empire has left significant Russian interests in the *near abroad*. One essential problem is the status of Russian settlers in the newly independent states, such as the Baltic states of Latvia and Estonia. These states want to limit Russian citizenship, and have set up language and electoral barriers to full Russian participation in Baltic lands. However, many ethnic Russians in these areas, including pre-World War II settlers, spouses of locals, and retired military personnel, have no other home. Ethnic Russians find themselves torn between denying their Russianness in order to assimilate into their adopted Baltic homeland, or exodus to an unknown Russian "homeland." For Balts, the Russian settlements that grew dramatically after World War II pose a problem for Baltic national identity. Thus, ethnic Russians and Balts alike have no easy solutions to decolonization.

In Ukraine, the largest of the new states, the substantial Russian population is pocketed in strategic territories, such as the mining region of Donetsk and the Crimean peninsula. Russians have long been essential to the local economy. These Russians naturally resist Ukrainian and other national de-Russification efforts. The strength of this Russian population was seen in the spring 1994 victory of a pro-Russian slate of candidates in local elections on the Crimean peninsula, as well as in the general Ukrainian elections of July 1994. In the case of Ukrainian-Russian relations—the most critical region of the *near abroad*—protracted

Ukraine

Reprinted from *The Newly Independent States of Eurasia: Handbook of Former Soviet Republics* by Stephen K. Batalden and Sandra L. Batalden, with permission from The Oryx Press, 4041 N. Central at Indian School Rd., Phoenix, AZ 85012, (800) 279-ORYX.

negotiations over the status of the Black Sea fleet and the Crimean peninsula continue. Especially troubling for Ukraine is Russia's military presence in the area.

Each day, the relationship between Russians and non-Russians is being fundamentally reshaped. Each of the fourteen new states of the *near abroad* has a unique population of Russians, nationals, and various minorities. Even before the USSR collapsed, Andrei Sakharov, the late Russian Nobel prizewinning nuclear physicist and human rights advocate, noted that the old republics of the Soviet Union were really "miniature empires."[8] Thus, each of Russia's new neighbors today is both a nation-state and a "miniature empire" that invariably contains one or more significant minority groups. For several of these new states, Russians are now the most prominent minority, fated to live outside the Russian Federation or to join the wave of returning Russians from the *near abroad.*

In the Soviet era, regional disputes between neighbors were moderated by Soviet political and military authority. The collapse of the Soviet Union in 1991 altered forever the relationships between empire and nation, between miniature empires and the autonomous regions within them, and between these newly independent states and their long-standing Russian populations. The new post-Soviet order in these matters is still being defined.

For Russians, however, the process of self-identification continues in a setting of profound cultural diversity. This diversity extends not only to the near abroad, but to the length and breadth of the Russian Federation itself.

Endnotes

[1] Translated by Valentine Snow in *Russian Intellectual History: An Anthology,* ed. by Marc Raeff. New York: Harcourt, Brace & World, 1966, pp. 167, 168.

[2] See Vera Tolz, "Thorny Road Toward Federalism in Russia," *RFE/RL Research Report,* December 3, 1993.

[3] "Treaty on the Delimitation of Spheres of Authority and the Mutual Delegation of Powers Between the Agencies of State Power of the Russian Federation and of the Republic of Tatarstan," *Rossiiskaia Gazeta,* February 17, 1994.

[4] N. B. Vakhtin, "Indigenous People of the Russian Far North: Land Rights and the Environment," unpublished paper delivered at United Nations Consultation on Indigenous Peoples, July 1993.

[5] Yevgeny Yevtushenko, *Divided Twins: Alaska and Siberia*, New York: Viking, 1988, p. 223.

[6] Michael Specter, "Siberia Awaits the Onslaught," *The New York Times*, September 4, 1994, p. 4E.

[7] Edward L. Keenan, "Rethinking the USSR, Now That It's Over," *The New York Times*, September 8, 1991.

[8] *Ogonek*, 1989, No. 31.

Suggested Readings

Batalden, Stephen K. and Sandra L. Batalden. *The Newly Independent States of Eurasia: Handbook of Former Soviet Republics*. Phoenix: The Oryx Press, 1993.

Bitov, Andrei. *A Captive of the Caucasus*, Susan Brownsberger tr. New York: Farrar, Straus, Giroux, 1992.

Critchlow, James. *Nationalism in Uzbekistan: A Soviet Republic's Road to Sovereignty*. Boulder, CO: Westview Press, 1991.

Feshbach, Murray and Alfred Friendly, Jr. *Ecocide in the USSR: Health and Nature Under Siege*. New York: Basic Books, 1992.

Forsyth, James. *A History of the Peoples of Siberia: Russia's North Asian Colony, 1581–1990*. Cambridge: Cambridge University Press, 1992.

Hosking, Geoffrey. *The Awakening of the Soviet Union*. Cambridge, MA: Harvard University Press, 1990.

Riasanovsky, Nicholas V. *A History of Russia*. 5th ed. New York: Oxford University Press, 1993.

Rorlich, Azade-Ayse. *The Volga Tatars: A Profile in National Resilience*. Stanford: Hoover Institution, 1986.

Vakhtin, Nikolai B. *Native Peoples of the Russian Far North*. London: Minority Rights Group, 1992.

Wixman, Ronald. *The Peoples of the USSR: An Ethnographic Handbook*. Armond, NY: M.E. Sharpe, 1984.

✑ʒ
Summary

The Dilemma of Being Russian as Viewed in the Historical Mirror

Max J. Okenfuss
Washington University, St. Louis, Missouri

The Roots of Russian Nationalism

The oldest documents of Russian history fairly bristle with two Christian ideas. These ideas were borrowed from the Greeks who gave them their faith. The first was: *united we stand, divided we fall.* When unified, the Christian princes of early Rus' were invincible, leading God's chosen people. Russian myth sanctified the ideas of cooperation and shared responsibility. The second idea was that Russia's conversion to Christianity was foreordained. Almost a thousand years ago, in the lands of ancient Rus'—centered today in Kiev in the newly independent Ukraine—Christian scribes announced that the East-Slavic peoples were essential to the divine plan. Old texts said that the land of Rus' was born when its people were brought under Christ's sway, strictly in conformity with Biblical prophesy. This prophesy ordained that their leader, St. Vladimir (ruled 980-1015), would accept Christianity and become wise above all men with his acceptance of the one true God.

The Christian message of a chosen people united under pious rulers is documented in Kiev's ancient chronicles, sermons, and saints' lives. In them, the individual was sublimated to the larger Christian community, and the prince was glorified. In Kiev today these texts are taken to be the heart of modern Ukraine nationalism. For the Ukrainians, they are proof that not only are they not Russians, they, not the Russians, were the chosen people.

These ideas were also embraced in the principality of Moscow, which became the modern state of Russia. Nearly half a millennium later, long after the decline of Kiev and the invasion of Eurasia by the Mongols, the same prophecy of a special, God-ordained, essentially spiritual role for the Russians was confiscated and embellished by the rising house of Moscow.

There, in the age of the European Renaissance and Reformation, these ideas formed the foundation for the future Russians' sense of self. This identification with a greater destiny was shared by peasant and prince alike. The tsars of Moscow began gathering the Russian lands, claiming a divine mission to do so. The old notion of Moscow as the Third Rome, referred to by Dr. Garrard, reflected this sense of destiny.

Centuries later, Russians became aware of the influence of modern Western civilization. Russians stood in awe of the wealth, industry, rationalism, and growing self-confidence of Europe. Some Russians said that their fate was to become European too, but few were prepared to abandon completely their inherited Christian notion that Russia had a special role in God's plan for humanity. Some suggested that Russia should imitate wholesale the European world. These people, who would renounce their unique Russianness in the name of economic progress or political fashion, were destined to become the most controversial monarchs and intellectuals in Russian history. Peter the Great was one. He announced a policy of imitation of Western military, political, and economic practices. Chaadaev, cited by Professor Batalden, was another who advocated imitation.

What exactly were the Russians' unique traits? Opinions varied widely, but nineteenth-century intellectuals, whether they were pro- or anti-European, tended to agree. Old Russia was a land of peaceful non-interference, while Europe was marked by war, rebellion, and big government. Europeans prided themselves on their intellects and science. Russians had religious faith and a divinely-appointed tsar. Europeans were rational. Russians were spontaneous. Europeans saw the world as lawful and predictable. Russians saw the intervening hand of a vengeful God.

Furthermore, prompted by their old sense of Christian mission, Russians felt vaguely that they were destined to teach their values to mankind. Some said, for example, that the Russian peasants' form of village organization should be exported to the rest of the world. Russian history, they claimed, was harmonious, while the West was marked by discord. Some intellectuals applauded, some condemned, but all recognized that the common people had preserved some innately Russian values and institutions which could be resurrected and taught to mankind.

At the beginning of this volume, I described Russia's modern social, economic, political and cultural revolutions, presided over by the last tsar, Nicholas II. Russia entered the twentieth century at least partially committed to the social equality, democracy, economic expansion, and even the individualism and constitutionalism of the modern West. But if Russia officially accepted this modern world, Russian society was unofficially divided by it. Russia was both urban and rural, rational and religious, European and Russian, Russian and non-Russian, Christian and non-Christian. Russia, to use Professor Stites' language, had by 1900 produced a popular culture in tension with its folk culture, and with the high culture of its elite.

Nicholas II was deeply disturbed by this fractured world he had helped create. His biographers report that Nicholas, while wearing the robes of state, was almost peasant-like. He was personally far more comfortable with the ancient spiritual bond between God, himself, and his chosen people, than he was with Western constitutional limits to his power. His susceptibility to Rasputin as an authentic, spiritual force mirrored his mental roots in the ancient faith of the Russian peasant. His desire to personally assume spiritual leadership of his armies during the First World War seems similarly rooted. Thus the last tsar was torn between the modern West and Russianness, between economic growth and religious faith, between popular culture and folk culture.

Surely, we would think, ancient folk myths and beliefs died with Nicholas' death at Bolshevik hands in 1918. They could not still survive today! Certainly the destruction of the Romanov dynasty, the Soviet world revolution, Communist dreams of a classless society, Stalin's brutal re-industrialization in innumerable Five-Year Plans, and successive Soviet constitutions put an end to these ancient Russian dreams. Surely the myths of Holy Russia could not have survived Gorbachev's *perestroika* and New World Order.

But survive they did, as Sergei Stankevich, adviser to Boris Yeltsin, affirmed in 1993:

> We must differentiate between Russia and the West. . . . From the early Middle Ages, Western societies have experienced a steady accretion of rationalism in their psychology and their institutions. . . . We had none of this. . . . Without my getting stereotypical, Russia's psychology is more spontaneous, unpredictable, artistic, more inclined to extremes of endless patience and explosions of license. . . . We can still have democracy, elections, a constitution, markets, and the rest, but if we intend to get anywhere we have to recognize our qualities—we have to recognize who we are and where we are starting from.[1]

Here is a Russian leader who is personally and politically guided and sustained by an inner sense of Russia's spiritual uniqueness and special mission. He rejects the idea that Russians are destined simply to become *like everyone else.*

One reason these old beliefs in Russia's uniqueness could survive was because of the official mythology created for the Russian Revolution of 1917. Although the tsar was dead, Russians were now told that theirs was the first of the inevitable revolutions that would bring the rest of the world into the workers' socialist paradise. Not only was their sense of a special mission preserved, but Russians discovered their precise contribution to mankind in scientific socialism. The death of Russian Christianity thus did not end the dream. Under the God-like Lenin, Russians retained a secularized version of their historic predestination that had sustained them under their Christian tsar.

(Independent Newspaper from Russia, Inc.)

In 1991, at the moment the Soviet Union was being dismantled, demonstrators looked to the past for political stability that was absent in their lives. Some, like the priest shown here, displayed a portrait of the family of the last tsar, Nicholas II. Others expressed their faith in the old Communist ideals, and held up a portrait of Lenin, the founder of the USSR.

Russian Nationalism Today

We cannot predict the fate of Yeltsin's political reforms. We cannot determine the success or failure of economic transformation, or even the territorial integrity of the new Russian Federation. But we can see that, at the close of the twentieth century, Russia confronts crossroads similar to those it faced at the beginning of the century. On the one hand, the "developed" outside world, the International Monetary Fund, reformers and democrats, Russia's private businessmen and Western investors all see Russia's future in markets, constitutions, civil liberties, and the unleashing of entrepreneurial talents. They are all committed to Russia's adoption of values pioneered by modern Europe and the West. Conversely, some feel that to be Russian is to be different from the rest of the world. They want to contribute something unique to world culture and social organization that is distinctly and undeniably Russian.

These are the Russian nationalists, whether or not they care about politics. Alexander Solzhenitsyn is a case in point. Perhaps no one has more consciously attempted to span Russia's cultures. His call to return to Russian spirituality made him *persona non grata* in the officially atheistic Soviet Union. As the Soviet Union was falling apart, he urged the creation of a new Russia, based upon Russian moral leadership of the ethnic East Slavs to whom the word of God was preached a thousand years ago. Even in the summer of 1994, upon his return after twenty years of exile, Solzhenitsyn called for a union of Russia, Ukraine, Belorussia, and a part of Kazakhstan. He dreamed of the resurrection of the military, economic, and historical integrity of the old Russian empire. Needless to say, Ukrainians, Belorussians, and others read events differently. So did Zhirinovsky, who told him to go back to the West, stating: *We don't need emigrants who sit there for 20 years and slander our people.*[2] But Solzhenitsyn echoed the deepest feelings of many, even those who disagreed with his political solutions.

Long before the Soviet Union broke into fourteen new nations, Russians complained that their Russianness was being destroyed by Communist cosmopolitanism. To the outside world, the USSR was Russia. The popular perception was that the Russian language and culture had been either brutally imposed upon, or willingly embraced by, the scores of peoples who made up the Soviet empire.

The reality was quite unlike the myth. In the Brezhnev and the Gorbachev eras, Russians increasingly felt that they had become second-class citizens. Other major nationalities had their own communist parties, but the Russians did not. Other nationalities had their own capitals, national anthems, encyclopedias, and academies of science, but not the Russians. Russian history had been suppressed in favor of Soviet history. Russians had the lowest birth rate, which extremists viewed as a form of self-annihilation. Russians disproportionately supported the rest of the USSR economically.[3] Long before Gorbachev, there was the beginning of a movement, a renaissance of Russian values, Russian spirituality, and Russian morality. The question was asked, why should Russians try to hold this union of ungrateful peoples together? The answer was a concession to nationalism that became the basis for the disintegration of the Soviet Union.

Anti-semitism was sometimes the ugly underside of this movement. Jews were blamed for the catastrophes in Russian history. The Jew Trotsky had led the October Revolution. A Jew had executed the last tsar. Solzhenitsyn himself had suggested that the infamous prison camps of the Gulag were Jewish inspired and Jewish led. Jews were responsible for the purges. Jews conspired to sell Russian artistic and religious treasures to the West. Even Gorbachev's *perestroika* was seen by extremists as a Jewish plot. His wife and closest advisers were described as Jews, half-Jews, or agents of Zionism. In blaming others, Russians could shift the responsibility away from themselves.

Combine this scapegoating with economic misery, and it is easy to see how the way was paved for such politicians as the notorious Vladimir Zhirinovsky. He has called for a return to the borders of the Russian empire of 1917. Time and again he challenges Russians to get off their knees. He demands that non-Russian announcers be removed from national television. He talks about recovering Russian Alaska. He awaits the day when the newly independent states beg to be readmitted to the Russian empire. On March 6, 1994, "60 Minutes" aired an interview in which Zhirinovsky said that the Russian parliament ought to announce a policy under which, should any Russian be killed in one of the fourteen new independent states, a native of that country would be executed. Should a Russian village be attacked, a native settlement would be razed. This is one of many voices of reemerging Russia that we are hearing. One of the great tragedies of our times is that the Western press is better at reporting on the personalities of outrageous nationalists like Zhirinovsky, than on the inner feelings and spiritual yearnings of those who are motivated to lend him support.

Not all voices of this Russian renaissance are so extreme. Not all are anti-semitic. Not all seek to reassert Russian leadership in world politics, as Yeltsin must in response to the nationalists. Many remain suspicious of the West's capitalist values, as shown in the following passage from a recent novel. This is the voice of a peasant:

> The main difference between the people and the bourgeoisie is that the people should not wish each other harm! The factory owner always wants his own factory to put his neighbor's factory out of business. That's understandable, but we aren't factory owners, are we? Or have this enmity and envy seeped into everyone's bones, sparing no one, neither tsar nor beggar?[4]

Echoed here is the ancient Russian notion that their peasants lived in a world of harmony and mutual non-interference with outsiders. By contrast, the implication is that the West was ruled by greed, capitalism, competition, and tensions, both among peoples and between them and their governments. Peasants further reject the sophisticated rationalism of the West:

> Thinking for a peasant was like swimming for a cow! Of course, a cow knows how to swim—if there is no other way to go. . . . A peasant can think, too, and sometimes he must, but to get lost in thought—absolutely not!

And as for the Western insistence on the equality of citizens, constitutions, and the values of democratic government, the novelist writes contemptuously:

> He's a smart one. He's happy words like 'democracy,' 'freedom and equality,' and 'duty and social consciousness' are being uttered even among the simple people. And while you're saying all these words to him, he'll shoot you first! Bang! 'Have a taste of democracy.'

Here a voice of the traditional Russian village, in a novel set in the years immediately after the Revolution, rejects the sacred institutions of alien Western culture. Like Peter the Great's opponents, he affirms that the Russian peasantry has preserved better, non-confrontational, unique alternatives.

But not only the politicians and the peasants are agitated. Agitation is the reality. Recently Igor Shafarevich, a right-wing intellectual said:

> Zhirinovsky is not the point. He is simply a vehicle to express our anger. For Russia right now the most important thing is to find a feeling of national unity to overcome this crisis. Today the main factor *is a total*

decline of national sentiments. We must have a leader who can unite Russia and Russians again. Zhirinovsky may disappear, but these ideas will not.[5]

In the last few years the Russian people have experienced devastating blows to their national pride. Critics have told them that they are the victims of mistaken Soviet history or of a Jewish conspiracy. They have seen their centuries-old empire collapse, and dozens of peoples within their shrunken borders have announced their independence and mistrust of Russians. Politicians scramble to hold the pieces together, and to reassert Russia's importance in the international arena. Within her own borders, concessions made to hold the Russian Federation together sound remarkably similar to despised former Soviet policies.

The Russians have lost their dominance over Eastern Europe, where millions are scurrying to forget Russian and learn German or English. Russians feel they have lost their leadership role in the world. The sudden collapse of their economy, the rise of lawlessness, the brazen swaggering and criminality of profiteer and mafia, and the retention of power and wealth by the old Communist elite—all invite conspiracy theories and scapegoating.

(*Independent Newspaper from Russia, Inc.*)

Disillusionment. Surviving veterans of World War II still wear the medals they were awarded for defending socialism and the motherland, and for defeating fascism and spreading Russian influence throughout Eastern Europe and around the globe. Now they must ask, why? Was their sacrifice for nothing?

Underlying these multiple shocks is the loss of a sense of national purpose. Worse than the loss of world leadership is the loss of the shared perception that Russians were destined in some way to lead, to contribute something special to humankind.

In these frightening conditions, some Russians are returning to thoughts a hundred and fifty years old:

> The principles underlying Russian culture are totally different from the competent elements of the culture of European peoples.... The Russian had nearly to destroy his national personality in order to assimilate Western civilization.[6]

They are rediscovering, as did intellectuals in the middle of the nineteenth century, an inner light that insists,

> *The essence of Russian civilization still lives on among the people.*
> *It will ... be possible for learning to develop in Russia on native principles, different from those which European culture offers us.*[7]

Confronted suddenly by Western consumerism, by Western greed, by crime in the streets, and by a profound loss of identity and destiny, some Russians today respond with dangerous nationalism.

The Humanities

If the view from the political arena is sometimes frightening, the Humanities give reason for hope. Russian artists, Professor Carlson reminds us, in liberating themselves from the imposed, insipid, Stalinist political dictates of Social Realism, not only ask what is Russian, but what is humane in the act of creativity? Reemerging from a world in which we scarcely knew that Soviet leaders had wives, Professor Clements tells us, Russian women are seeking liberated new roles in family life, in the work-place, and in politics. They have been promised much, but given little in the last seventy years. Much Russian film is returning to its early twentieth-century roots, Professor Youngblood tells us, but that creates a battleground, since many reject Americanization out of hand. Whether showing the Hollywood films preferred by the public, or creating new ones, Russian cinema today is visually and vividly questioning conventions, exploring Russia's place in the world, and showing perspectives not visible without the camera's close-up vision. It has the capacity to entertain, to stir up anti-foreign sentiments, or to flatter national pride.

Literature is perhaps the most promising arena, we are told by Professors Weil and Vishevsky. The resurgence of Russian literature, perhaps the most boldly rebellious of the arts under the Soviet regime, has a powerful voice. The lively Russian literary scene and the continuing popularity of live Russian poetry readings suggest that Russian national pride has much to celebrate. Ordinary Russians can finally identify with the international literary acclaim accorded to writers like Nabokov, Pasternak, and Solzhenitsyn.

Tolstoy once said: *The aims of the artist are incompatible with social goals. Artists don't solve problems . . ., they make people love life.* He echoed Chekhov, who wrote, *It would be nice to combine art with preaching, but for me it is . . . virtually impossible.* In the Soviet Union, however, writers mirrored their world, struggled against evil, preserved hope, and kept the common people in touch with their culture. Writers have also, particularly in contemporary literature, lost hope, abandoned dreams, and forced their readers to confront the abyss of reality.

Russia and its bordering neighbors are a morass of ethnic complicities. On the one hand, Professor Batalden informs us, Russia's nearest neighbors and former subjects defiantly define themselves as non-Russian. It is in their leaders' political interest to do so. On the other hand, every new nation on the borders is a miniature empire, containing significant numbers of Russians, whom some Russian nationalists have sworn to protect or recover. The Crimea is a case in point. With a considerable Russian population, the area belongs to Ukraine, although few Ukrainian speakers live there. Its ports are home to a fleet essential to Ukrainian prestige, but claimed by Russia. Once home to peoples deported by Stalin, the region is subject to a re-migration of Tatars and Germans who want to reclaim land, homes, and businesses. It remains to be seen whether extremist Russian nationalists will push political leaders into postures dangerous for Russia, her neighbors, and the world, or whether the reemerging feeling of Russianness will remain cultural and non-political.

The outside world faces equally perilous choices. If it insists upon a speedy and enthusiastic Russian transformation to the world marketplace, it risks a predictable nationalist reaction that could destroy reform. If America and other developed nations support caution and moderation in economic change, they risk prolonging or intensifying an economic crisis which also feeds nationalist extremists.

We take it for granted that our economy is interlocked with that of the rest of the world, subject to constant interventions and readjustments. To Russians, only recently liberated from an ideology which daily preached the evils of Western capitalism, a national economy manipulated by American capitalists, by the invisible financial forces of Zurich, by Japanese monopolists, or by the mafia, is a scary thought.

Finally, reemerging Russia faces not only religious rebirth, but also the religious crises described by Dr. Garrard. Russians of all ages flock to church services, celebrating the demise of official atheism. Russians, including Solzhenitsyn, joyfully resurrect the idea of a holy Russia based on the Orthodox Church. That Church, however, is mistrusted by many believers, for it survived only by collaborating with the Soviet state. Other Christian religions in Europe and America, long hostile to Soviet atheism, have enthusiastically offered alternatives to religiously deprived Russians. Their missionary activity, in person and on television, has in turn led to angry protests by the Orthodox hierarchy, and by Russian nationalists, who see only further Americanization.

Furthermore Orthodoxy doesn't have just "one" voice. In 1994 in St. Petersburg the Metropolitan Iov is a far-right neo-conservative critic of Boris Yeltsin. In Moscow the Patriarch Aleksei opened governmental sessions, sanctioned governmental policies, and indeed proved invaluable to the government during the coups of August 1991, and October, 1993. This complex tangle of politics and religion raises questions.

A paradox arises. At first glance Orthodoxy could buttress the new Russia. No single idea, however, is so threatening to reemerging Russia as the original idea of holy Russia. If Orthodoxy becomes linked to the new Russian Federation, it could feed separatist sentiments of largely Islamic regions which contain Russia's reserves of gold, diamonds, and oil. If Orthodoxy and Russian nationalism merge, not only would Russians become further divided, they could find themselves in conflict with their ethnic brothers. Ukrainians are already divided between Russian Orthodox, Uniate, and Ukrainian Orthodox Churches, all seeking the minds, hearts, and the church properties of Ukraine. If Russian Orthodoxy genuinely reemerged, with its emphasis on the divine mission of the Russians, with its inherent susceptibility to anti-Semitism, anti-Catholicism, and anti-Protestantism, Russia's place in the world community would be called into question as much as was Red Russia's in 1917.

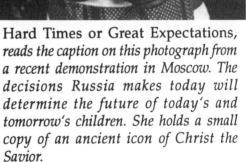

(Photograph by Mark Shteinbok from *Independent Newspaper from Russia.*, Inc.)

Hard Times or Great Expectations, *reads the caption on this photograph from a recent demonstration in Moscow. The decisions Russia makes today will determine the future of today's and tomorrow's children. She holds a small copy of an ancient icon of Christ the Savior.*

The question is not whether Russians rediscover religion, but whether Russia becomes officially religious. Traditional Russian Orthodoxy, it is generally conceded, was more an annual cycle of rites and rituals than a set of guidelines to guide the behavior of an educated society. It is unlikely to form the essential basis of a new Russian sense of identity or mission.

(Photograph by Dimity Borko from Independent Newspaper from Russia, Inc.)

In 1993, Russian voters narrowly approved a federal constitution for the new Russia. The world press and international observers watched closely.

So what holds a nation together? In 1993 the various peoples of Russia narrowly approved a federal constitution. It will not guide them unaltered a century or even a decade from now. It has only been a few years since Gorbachev first announced *perestroika*, and fewer still since the collapse of the Soviet Union. At the birth of the United States, seventeen years and a war elapsed between the Declaration of Independence and the adoption of the Constitution with its first ten amendments. A few years ago, Yugoslavia had the longest constitution in the world. It didn't work. Constitutions are only guidelines for societies. They do not, in and of themselves, hold a nation together.

In the middle of the nineteenth century, when modern nations and modern nationalism were being born in Europe and old empires were under attack, a French historian offered a simple formula: *A nation is the will to live together*.[8] No nation is ethnically, culturally, linguistically, religiously homogeneous. None of the twentieth century's horrors—ethnic cleansing, self-determination, elections, death camps, deportation, purges—could create a society in which all men and all women were equal, united, and always in agreement.

A nation is the will to live together. In Professor Stites' words that opened this volume, a nation is the willingness of the majority of people representing the high, popular, and folk cultures in a land to accept, to tolerate, to celebrate, the humanity of others in their land. That will to live together is sorely tested in reemerging Russia.

Endnotes

[1] David Remnik, "Yeltsin's Tightrope," *The New Yorker*, May 10, 1993, p. 82.

[2] *St. Louis Post Dispatch*, July 22, 1994.

[3] Here and below I follow the observations of Richard Hellie, "Muscovy Redux," *Russian History*, Vol. 17, No. 4, esp. pp. 422-424.

[4] Ibid.

[5] Michael Specter, " The Great Russia Will Live Again," *The New York Times*, June 19, 1994, p.56.

[6] Ibid.

[7] Ivan Vasil'evich Kireevski, in Marc Raeff, *Russian Intellectual History*, pp. 180, 206-7.

[8] Cited by Helene Carrere d'Encausse. *Decline of an Empire*. New York: Newsweek Books, 1974.

Suggested Readings

Billington, James. *The Icon and the Axe*, New York: Knopf, 1966.

Cherniavsky, Michael. *Tsar and People*, New York: Random House, 1961.

Laqueur, Walter. *Black Hundred*. New York: Harper Collins, 1993.

Pipes, Richard. *Russia Under the Old Regime*. New York: Scribners, 1974.

Raeff, Marc. *Russian Intellectual History. An Anthology*. New York: Harcourt Brace, 1966.

Remnik, David. *Lenin's Tomb*. New York: Random House, 1993.

Riasanovsky, Nicholas V. *A History of Russia*, 5th ed. Oxford: Oxford University Press, 1993.

About the Authors

Stephen K. Batalden is professor of history and coordinator of the Russian and East European Studies Consortium at Arizona State University. He received his Ph.D. (1975) and M.A. (1972) from the University of Minnesota. His publications, including the recent edited volume, *Seeking God* (DeKalb, 1993), and the co-authored study, *The Newly Independent States of Eurasia* (Phoenix, 1993), explore the issues at the interface of religious and ethnic identification in Russian culture.

Maria Carlson is presently the Director of the Center for Russian and East European Studies at the University of Kansas. After receiving her Ph.D. in Russian Literature from Indiana University in 1981, she lived in Moscow for six years, where she continued her research into Russian intellectual history, culture and literature. In 1987 she returned to teach at the University of Kansas and in 1992 received the University's prestigious H. Bernerd Fink Award for Outstanding Classroom Teaching. She has written 15 articles and given more than 50 professional and popular presentations on Russian thought, culture, art, and literature. She is the author of a book on the Russian Theosophical Movement, *'No Religion Higher than Truth:' A History of the Theosophical Movement in Russia 1875–1922* (1993). Russian art is both her professional and personal passion.

Barbara Evans Clements grew up in Richmond, Virginia. She received her B.A. from the University of Richmond, and her M.A. and Ph.D. from Duke University. Currently she is a professor of history at the University of Akron, where she teaches European history , as well as the history of women. She has concentrated her research on Russian women in the late imperial and early Soviet periods. She is the author of scholarly books and articles, among them *Bolshevik Feminist: The Life of Aleksandra Kollontai* (1979).

Carol Garrard received her Ph.D. from the University of Virginia in English Literature. After teaching in the Virginia Community College System for ten years, she became a full-time writer. With her husband John, Professor of Russian Literature at the University of Arizona, she has co-authored many articles on Russian and Soviet literature, as well as *Inside the Soviet Writers' Union* (1990), *World War II and the Soviet People* (1993, editor and contributor) and *Stepson in the Motherland: Vasily Grossman and the Holocaust* (scheduled for publication April 1995). The Garrards are active volunteers for the southern Arizona Holocaust Education Committee.

Max J. Okenfuss (Ph.D. Harvard, 1971) associate professor of History at Washington University, is Project Director for the *Reemerging Russia* program. He has published *The Discovery of Childhood in Russia* (1980), and *The Travel*

Diary of Peter Tolstoi (1987). His *Rise and Fall of Latin Humanism in Early-Modern Russia* is scheduled for publication in 1995. He is also the American Editor of the *Jahrbücher für Geschichte Osteuropas*.

Richard Stites (Ph.D. Harvard, 1968), professor of History at Georgetown University, is senior humanist for the *Reemerging Russia* program. He has pioneered and is today recognized as the leading American scholar of popular culture in late Imperial Russia and of the unofficial culture of the Soviet Union. He is the author of *The Women's Liberation Movement in Russia: Feminism, Nihilism, and Bolshevism, 1860-1930* (1978, rev. ed. 1990), and more recently of *Revolutionary Dreams: Utopian Vision and Experimental Life in the Russian Revolution* (1989), and *Russian Popular Culture: Entertainment and Society Since 1900* (1992).

Anatoly Vishevsky is assistant professor of Russian at Grinnell College and is also Associate Director of Middlebury College Russian Summer School. He earned his M.A. in English from the University of Chernovtsy, Ukraine. He left the Ukraine in 1980, and in 1985 he received his Ph.D. in Russian Literature from the University of Kansas. He has published a number of articles, primarily on twentieth-century Russian literature, and a scholarly book *Soviet Literary Culture of the 1970s: The Politics of Irony* (1993). He is also a co-author (with Boris Briker) of *The Dod's Affair* (1983), a collection of short stories in Russian.

Irwin Weil is professor of Russian Languages and Literature at Northwestern University, where he has been teaching since 1966. He received his A.B. and M.A. at the University of Chicago, and his Ph.D. at Harvard. Every year, for thirty-five years, he has gone to the former USSR, now Russia, to teach in Russian universities, work and lecture at the Academy of Sciences, and organize cultural and musical events in Russian public life and on Russian television. He has accumulated intimate knowledge of Russian events from many different political periods, and has a great collection of Russian songs, which he performs in the U.S. and Russia. His publications cover different aspects of Russian, Soviet, and Jewish cultures.

Denise J. Youngblood, a specialist in Russian social and cultural history, is an associate professor of history at the University of Vermont. She received her Ph.D. from Stanford University and studied film at the State Institute of Cinematography, Moscow. She has written widely on Soviet film, including many articles and two books, *Soviet Cinema in the Silent Era, 1918–1935* (1991) and *Movies for the Masses: Popular Cinema and Soviet Society in the 1920s* (1992). She is currently at work on a book about the pre-revolutionary Russian movie industry.

Glossary

Akhmatova, Anna (1888–1966): gifted Russian poet and heroine of Russian intellectual life; author of *Requiem Part II for Leningrad*

Aksyonov, Vassily (1932–): contemporary Russian writer

Alternative Literature: contemporary Russian literature that breaks from anything associated with previous literature

anarchist: person who rebels against political authority

anti-semitic: against Jews, their traits, attributes or customs

artnost': freedom to create art unbound by official sanctions

autonomous: independent of the laws of another state or government; self-governing

avant-garde: a group of writers and artists regarded as preeminent in the invention and application of new techniques in a given field

Bakst, Leonid (1866–1924): Russian Symbolist artist

Bely, Andrei (1880–1934): Russian Symbolist writer

Benois, Alexander (1870–1960): Russian Symbolist artist

Berdiaev, Nicholas: Russian philosopher

Black Marias: people were taken away by the secret police in these vehicles

Blok, Alexander (1850–1921): Russian Symbolist writer

Bolsheviks: participants in the Russian Revolution belonging to the Communist Party of the Soviet Union; members of the left-wing majority group of the Russian Social Democratic Party adopting Lenin's thesis on party organization (1903)

bourgeois: belonging to or typical of the middle classes; having self-centered, materialistic and conformist ideas

Brezhnev, Leonid Ilyich (1906–1982): Russian statesman, first secretary of the Soviet Union Communist Party (1964–1982)

censer: an incense vessel

Briusov, Valery (1873–1924): Russian Symbolist writer

Brodsky, Isaak (1884–1939): Russian representational artist

Bulatov, Erik (1933–): contemporary Russian artist

Bulgakov, Mikhail (1891–1940): Russian novelist and dramatist

Bulgakova, Olga (1951–): contemporary Russian artist

Cezanne, Paul (1839–1906): French painter

Chaadaev, Peter (1794–1856): Russian philosopher and intellectual

Chagall, Marc (1887–1985): French painter of Russian-Jewish origin, a rich colorist with great poetic imagination, often taking subjects from Russian village life or Jewish folklore and religion

Chekhov, Anton Pavolvich (1860–1904): Russian dramatist and short-story writer. His most famous plays are *The Seagull* (1895), *Uncle Vanya* (1900), The *Three Sisters* (1901) and *The Cherry Orchard* (1903)

Citation Art: using this modernist concept, a painter may consciously incorporate images, references, associations, color symbolism, or other emblems in the painting, inviting the sophisticated viewer to associate them with other works from different times and places; thus, expanding the meaning of the painting through association

Cold War: the state of political tension and military rivalry between the Soviet and American blocs of nations following World War II

communism: the ownership of property, or means of production, distribution and supply, by the whole of a classless society, with wealth shared on the principle of "to each according to his need, from each according to his ability"

Communism: a social and political movement which is based on Marx's interpretation of history and which seeks to achieve communism by revolutionary means

Critical Realists: artists and writers of Critical Realism, the purpose of which was to activate the Russian's social conscience and show them how to live moral and useful lives

Deineka, Alexander (1899–1969): Russian representational artist

Diaghilev, Sergei Pavlovich (1872–1929): Russian ballet impresario; developed the famous Russian Ballet

Diocletian: Gaius Aurelius Valerius Diocletianus, A.D. 245–313; Roman emperor (A.D. 284–305)

doggerel: trivial verse composed in loose form

Dostoyevsky, Fyodor Mikhailovich (1821–1881): Russian novelist. His greatest works, written in his last 17 years, include *Crime and Punishment* (1866), *The Idiot* (1858–1859) and *The Brothers Karamazov* (1880). The peculiarly Dostoyevskian situation is the anguish of a character suspended between systems of belief calling for separate courses of action

Duma: Russian nationalist parliament, convened and dissolved four times between 1905 and 1917

Eisenstein, Sergei Mikhailovich (1898–1948): Russian film director. He perfected the techniques of cutting and close-up in *Strike* (1923), *The Battleship Potemkin* (1925) and *October* (1928)

émigré: an emigrant, especially one who has fled his country during a revolution

federation: a joining together of states in a union that recognizes local autonomy

Fedotov, Pavel (1815–1852): Russian Critical Realist painter

folk culture: produced in the tradition of the common people that make up a nation, e.g. farmers, peasants.

fourth dimension: the dimension (time) added in the space-time continuum to the three spatial dimensions

fratricidal: driven to killing one's brother or sister

glasnost': new policy of openness promoted by Mikhail Gorbachev which allowed public scrutiny of the Soviet government and sparked a new cultural revolution

Goethe, Johann Wolfgang von (1749–1832): German poet, dramatist and novelist

Golovin, Alexander (1863–1930): Russian Symbolist artist

Gerasimov, Sergei (1885–1964): Russian Socialist Realism painter

Goncharov, Ivan Aleksandrovich (1812–1891): Russian novelist, author of *Oblomov* (1857), a picture of the indolent Russian country gentleman

Gorbachev, Mikhail Sergeyevich (1931–): Soviet Communist Party general secretary and president (1985–1991); educated in law and agriculture, he succeeded Konstantin Chernenko as Soviet leader in 1985 and worked toward improved Soviet social and economic conditions and better relations with Western countries. He projected the new image of younger leadership in the USSR and promoted *glasnost'* (openness) and *perestroika* (restructuring)

Gorky, Maxim (1868–1936): (Aleksei Maksimovich Peshkov) Russian author

high culture: fine art, classical music, legitimate theater, ballet, opera and classical studies

Ibsen, Henrik Johan (1828–1906): Norwegian dramatist

icon: a representation of a sacred Christian personage, itself regarded as sacred, especially in the tradition of the Eastern Churches

idiom: a regional speech or dialect; a specialized vocabulary used by a group of people; jargon

indigenous: native; occurring or living naturally in an area, not introduced

inostrantsy: special Russian vocabulary in reference to non-Russians living outside the Empire, in this case meaning foreigners, those from another country

inorodtsy: special Russian vocabulary in reference to non-Russians living within the Empire, in this case meaning those of other birth

inovertsy: special Russian vocabulary in reference to non-Russians, in this case meaning those of other faith

Kandinsky, Wassily (1866–1944): Russian painter; naturalized German (1928) then French (1939). Painting free, spontaneous forms using color and line alone for their expressive power, his work strongly influenced abstract expressionism

near abroad: the fourteen new republics created in the Confederation of Independent States which resulted from the collapse of the USSR in 1991

Kabakov, Ilya (1933–): contemporary Russian artist

Khrushchev, Nikita Sergeyevich (1894–1971): First secretary of the Russian Communist Party (1953–1964); premier of the Soviet Union (1958–1964)

Komar, Vitaly (1943–): contemporary Russian artist, previously a counter-culture artist

Kremlinologist: an expert on the workings and the thinking of Soviet internal and external politics

Kropotkin, Prince Pyotr Alekseyevich (1842–1921): Russian social philosopher and anarchist.

Kuleshov, Lev: Soviet film director and film theorist

Lunacharsky, Anatoly: Russian Commissar of Enlightenment (Secretary of Education and Culture) in the 1920s

Malevich, Kasimir (1878–1935): Russian painter and sculptor whose geometric abstractions culminated in a white square on a white background in *White on White* (1919)

Mandelshtam, Nadezhda: wife of Osip Mandelshtam; after his death, published two books of her own memoirs that included some of his poetry

Mandelshtam, Osip (1892–1938): Russian poet who fell out of favor with the terrorist police; he was exiled in the 1930s, then later, arrested and placed in a camp where he perished

Manifest Destiny: in U.S. history, the nineteenth-century doctrine that the United States had the right and duty to expand throughout the North American continent

Marxist: one who believes in or follows the ideas of Karl Marx, German philosopher and founder of world Communism, and Friedrich Engels, German socialist leader, writer and collaborator with Marx; a militant Communist

Matisse, Henri (1869–1954): French painter and sculptor, leader of the Fauves, and early 20th-century liberating movement in painting in France

Mayakovsky, Vladimir Vladimirovich (1893–1930): Russian poet and playwright. He glorified the revolution, in verse remarkable for its verbal invention, wordplay, etc.

Melamid, Alexander (1945–): contemporary Russian artist, previously a counter-culture artist

Nabokov, Vladimir (1899–1977): Russo-American novelist

Nazarenko, Tatiana (1944–): contemporary Russian artist

Neizvestny, Ernst (1955–): contemporary Russian artist, previously a counter-culture artist

New Economic Policy (NEP): The program in the USSR between 1921 and 1928 whereby concessions were made to capitalism in small industry, retail trade and agriculture

Nicholas II: Nikolai Aleksandrovich (1868–1918) tsar of Russia; succeeded Alexander III; abdicated in 1917; executed with his family at Ekaterinburg in 1918

Nietzsche, Friedrich Wilhelm (1844–1900): German philosopher, philologist and poet

novella: a short prose tale; a short novel

Orlova, Lyubov: Russian female movie star of the 1930s

Peter the Great: tsar of Russia (1672–1725)

Pasternak, Boris Leonidovich (1890–1960): Russian writer, author of *Dr. Zhivago* (1958) and winner of the Nobel Prize for Literature (1958)

perestroika: restructuring, new thinking, new approach to government; used by Mikhail Gorbachev as the title of his book, it signaled a fundamental change in the political, economic, social, and cultural policies of the Soviet government

Perov, Vasily (1833–1882): Russian Critical Realist painter

Petrov-Vodkin, Kuzma (1878–1939): Russian representational artist

Pharisaism: hypocritical observance of the letter of religious or moral law without regard for the spirit; sanctimoniousness

pogrom: an organized and often officially encouraged massacre or persecution of a minority group, especially one conducted against the Jews

Pimenov, Yuri (1903–1977): Russian representational artist

Plastov, Arkadii (1893–1972): Russian Socialist Realism painter

Popov, Evgeny (1946–): Russian writer

popular culture: urban culture produced for a mass audience

Pushkin, Alexander Sergeievich (1799–1837): Russian poet, novelist and short-story writer

Rasputin, Grigori Efimovich (1817?–1916): Russian mystic monk who was assassinated; favorite of the imperial family (Nicholas II)

rationalism: the theory that the exercise of reason, rather than the acceptance of empiricism, authority, or spiritual revelation, provides the only valid basis for action or belief, and that reason is the prime source of knowledge and of spiritual truth

Reed, John (1887–1920): American journalist and poet, eye-witness to the Revolution of 1917

Riangina, Serafima (1891–1955): Russian Socialist Realism painter

Repin, Ilya (1844–1930): Russian Critical Realist painter

repression epigonism: an art form which expresses nostalgia for itself and repeats already developed themes; second rate imitation art

Rodchenko, Alexander (1891–1956): Russian avant-garde artist

Roerich, Nikolai (1874–1947): Russian Symbolist artist

Romanov: the Russian ruling dynasty from the accession (1613) of Michael until the forced abdication (1917) of Nicholas II

Russian Silver Age (1890–1915): in the two decades that preceded the Revolution of 1917, Russia experienced a flowering of the graphic and decorative arts unprecedented in history; partly a reaction against the social messages and the civic art of the Critical Realists; the themes of the Silver Age were love and death, the demonic, folklore, mythology and a romanticized and idealized Russian past

Russophile: person who admires Russia or Russian civilization

Scriabin, Alexander (1871/72–1915): Russian composer

semitism: Jewish traits, attributes or customs

Shaw, George Bernard (1856–1950): Irish playwright and critic

shock workers (*ugaruik*): term used in Soviet industry to indicate the most aggressive people carrying out Party policy; *ugaruik* was also used for 'shock troops' the most elite, frontline soldiers

Shukshin, Vasili (1929–1974): Russian writer and film director

Slav: a member of a group of Eastern European peoples, usually subdivided into Eastern Slavs (Great Russians, Ukrainians and Belorussians), Western Slavs (e.g. Poles, Moravians, Czechs, Slovaks) and Southern Slavs (e.g. Serbs, Croats, Slovenes, Bulgars)

Slavic: of the Slavs, their languages, etc.; a major branch of the Indo-European family of languages

Socialist Realism: didactic use of the arts for the development of social consciousness and the enhancement of the socialist state

Solov'iev, Vladimir (1853–1900): Russian religious and mystical philosopher

Solzhenitsyn, Aleksandr (1918–): Soviet writer. In his novels, including *One Day in the Life of Ivan Deniscovich* (1962), *Cancer Ward* (1968) and *The First Circle* (1968) he describes the injustice and degradation suffered by millions of Russians in the Stalinist concentration camps. Winner of the Nobel Prize (1970)

Sorokin, Vladimir: contemporary Russian writer

Stalin, Joseph (1879–1953): general secretary of the Communist Party of the Soviet Union (1922–1953); premier (1941–1953)

Stanislavsky, Konstantin (1863–1938): Russian theatrical producer. Founder of the Moscow Art Theater (1896), he developed a new approach to acting and production based on realism, ensemble acting, and the actor's complete identification with his character

Stravinsky, Igor (1882–1971): Russian composer, naturalized French (1934), then American (1945)

Surikov, Vasily (1848–1916): Russian Critical Realist painter

Symbolist Painters: artists who employed stylization and design for their own sake, creating a dreamier, more impressionistic style, with color applied as fuzzy patches in order to catch mood and light rather than represent an object; Themes of the Symbolists painters were echoed in the works of writers, clothing and furniture designers, architects, craftsmen, composers and philosophers

taiga: the subarctic evergreen forest of Siberia and of similar regions elsewhere in Eurasia and North America

Tatlin, Vladimir (1885–1953): Russian avant-garde artist

Thaw: the liberalization in political and cultural life in the Soviet Union following Stalin's death in 1953

theocracy: government and religion intertwined with the governmental ruler also functioning as the religious leader

Tolstoy, Count Leo Nikolayevich (1828–1910): Russian novelist and moral philosopher. Best known for his two masterpieces, *War and Peace* (1864–1869) and *Anna Karenina* (1875–1877)

totalitarianism: using policies whose main characteristic is absolute monarchy; tyrannical

Trotsky, Leon (1879–1940): Russian revolutionist who played a leading role in bringing the Bolsheviks to power

tsar: variant of czar, one of the former emperors of Russia

tsarist: in popular usage, an autocratic system of government

Tsvetaeva, Marina (1892–1941): Russian poet who emigrated to Western Europe in the 1920s, but returned to the Soviet Union in 1939 only to be exiled to the provinces where she committed suicide

Turgenev, Ivan Sergeyevich (1818–1883): Russian writer. His work was unpopular in official circles, partly because of his liberal Western tendencies. *A Sportsman's Sketches* (1852), a collection of stories of peasant life, was an impassioned plea for the abolition of serfdom. He influenced Chekhov and through him European literature as a whole.

uncial: a style of writing characterized by somewhat rounded capital letters; found especially in Greek and Latin manuscripts of the fourth to the eighth centuries A.D.

Vrubel, Mikhail (1856–1910): Russian Symbolist artist

Vysotski, Vladimir (1938–1980): Russian poet, songwriter and bard

Witte, Count Sergei Yulievich (1849–1915): Russian statesman. As minister of finance, commerce and industry (1892–1903) he introduced the gold standard and opened up Siberia by the Trans-Siberian Railroad; prime minister (1905–1906)

Yeltsin, Boris (1931–): Russian Federation President (1991–)

Yevtushenko, Yevgeny: modern Russian poet

Young Prose: Russian literary movement of the 1950s and early 1960s

Zhirinovsky, Vladimir (1946–): Russian right-wing political leader and head of the Liberal Democratic Party

Index